Travel phrasebooks collection
«Everything Will Be Okay!»

PHRASEBOOK

— SERBIAN —

THE MOST IMPORTANT PHRASES

This phrasebook contains the most important phrases and questions for basic communication Everything you need to survive overseas

By Andrey Taranov

T&P BOOKS

Phrasebook + 1500-word dictionary

English-Serbian phrasebook & concise dictionary

By Andrey Taranov

The collection of "Everything Will Be Okay" travel phrasebooks published by T&P Books is designed for people traveling abroad for tourism and business. The phrasebooks contain what matters most - the essentials for basic communication. This is an indispensable set of phrases to "survive" while abroad.

Another section of the book also provides a small dictionary with more than 1,500 useful words arranged alphabetically. The dictionary includes a lot of gastronomic terms and will be helpful when ordering food at a restaurant or buying groceries at the store.

T&P Books Publishing
www.tpbooks.com

ISBN: 978-1-78492-433-1

This book is also available in E-book formats.
Please visit www.tpbooks.com or the major online bookstores.

FOREWORD

The collection of "Everything Will Be Okay" travel phrasebooks published by T&P Books is designed for people traveling abroad for tourism and business. The phrasebooks contain what matters most - the essentials for basic communication. This is an indispensable set of phrases to "survive" while abroad.

This phrasebook will help you in most cases where you need to ask something, get directions, find out how much something costs, etc. It can also resolve difficult communication situations where gestures just won't help.

This book contains a lot of phrases that have been grouped according to the most relevant topics. A separate section of the book also provides a small dictionary with more than 1,500 important and useful words.

Take "Everything Will Be Okay" phrasebook with you on the road and you'll have an irreplaceable traveling companion who will help you find your way out of any situation and teach you to not fear speaking with foreigners.

TABLE OF CONTENTS

T&P Books Publishing

PRONUNCIATION

Letter	Serbian example	T&P phonetic alphabet	English example

Vowels

А а	авлија	[a]	shorter than in ask
Е е	ексер	[e]	elm, medal
И и	излаз	[i]	shorter than in feet
О о	очи	[o]	pod, John
У у	ученик	[u]	book

Consonants

Б б	брег	[b]	baby, book
В в	вода	[ʋ]	vase, winter
Г г	глава	[g]	game, gold
Д д	дим	[d]	day, doctor
Ђ ђ	ђак	[ʤ]	jeans, gene
Ж ж	жица	[ʒ]	forge, pleasure
З з	зец	[z]	zebra, please
Ј ј	мој	[j]	yes, New York
К к	киша	[k]	clock, kiss
Л л	лептир	[l]	lace, people
Љ љ	љиљан	[ʎ]	daily, million
М м	мајка	[m]	magic, milk
Н н	нос	[n]	name, normal
Њ њ	књига	[ɲ]	canyon, new
П п	праг	[p]	pencil, private
Р р	рука	[r]	rice, radio
С с	слово	[s]	city, boss
Т т	тело	[t]	tourist, trip
Ћ ћ	ћуран	[ʨ]	cheer
Ф ф	фењер	[f]	face, food
Х х	хлеб	[h]	home, have
Ц ц	цео	[ʦ]	cats, tsetse fly
Ч ч	чизме	[ʧ]	church, French

Letter	Serbian example	T&P phonetic alphabet	English example
Џ џ	џбун	[dʒ]	joke, general
Ш ш	шах	[ʃ]	machine, shark

LIST OF ABBREVIATIONS

English abbreviations

ab.	-	about
adj	-	adjective
adv	-	adverb
anim.	-	animate
as adj	-	attributive noun used as adjective
e.g.	-	for example
etc.	-	et cetera
fam.	-	familiar
fem.	-	feminine
form.	-	formal
inanim.	-	inanimate
masc.	-	masculine
math	-	mathematics
mil.	-	military
n	-	noun
pl	-	plural
pron.	-	pronoun
sb	-	somebody
sing.	-	singular
sth	-	something
v aux	-	auxiliary verb
vi	-	intransitive verb
vi, vt	-	intransitive, transitive verb
vt	-	transitive verb

Serbian abbreviations

ж	-	feminine noun
ж мн	-	feminine plural
м	-	masculine noun
м мн	-	masculine plural
мн	-	plural
с	-	neuter
с мн	-	neuter plural

SERBIAN
PHRASEBOOK

This section contains
important phrases that may
come in handy in various
real-life situations.
The phrasebook will help
you ask for directions, clarify
a price, buy tickets, and
order food at a restaurant

T&P Books Publishing

PHRASEBOOK CONTENTS

T&P Books Publishing

The bare minimum

Excuse me, …	**Извините, …** Izvinite, …
Hello.	**Добар дан.** Dobar dan
Thank you.	**Хвала вам.** Hvala vam
Good bye.	**Довиђења.** Doviđenja
Yes.	**Да.** Da
No.	**Не.** Ne
I don't know.	**Не знам.** Ne znam
Where? | Where to? | When?	**Где? | Куда? | Када?** Gde? | Kuda? | Kada?

I need …	**Треба ми …** Treba mi …
I want …	**Хоћу …** Hoću …
Do you have …?	**Имате ли …?** Imate li …?
Is there a … here?	**Да ли овде постоји …?** Da li ovde postoji …?
May I …?	**Смем ли …?** Smem li …?
…, please (polite request)	**молим** molim

I'm looking for …	**Тражим …** Tražim …
restroom	**тоалет** toalet
ATM	**банкомат** bankomat
pharmacy (drugstore)	**апотеку** apoteku
hospital	**болницу** bolnicu
police station	**полицијску станицу** policijsku stanicu
subway	**метро** metro

| taxi | **такси**
taksi |
| train station | **железничку станицу**
železničku stanicu |

My name is ...	**Ја се зовем ...** Ja se zovem ...
What's your name?	**Како се ви зовете?** Kako se vi zovete?
Could you please help me?	**Да ли бисте, молим вас, могли да ми помогнете?** Da li biste, molim vas, mogli da mi pomognete?
I've got a problem.	**Имам проблем.** Imam problem
I don't feel well.	**Не осећам се добро.** Ne osećam se dobro
Call an ambulance!	**Позовите хитну помоћ!** Pozovite hitnu pomoć!
May I make a call?	**Смем ли да телефонирам?** Smem li da telefoniram?

| I'm sorry. | **Извините ...**
Izvinite ... |
| You're welcome. | **Нема на чему.**
Nema na čemu |

I, me	**ја, мене** ja, mene
you (inform.)	**ти** ti
he	**он** on
she	**она** ona
they (masc.)	**они** oni
they (fem.)	**оне** one
we	**ми** mi
you (pl)	**ви** vi
you (sg, form.)	**ви** vi

ENTRANCE	**УЛАЗ** ULAZ
EXIT	**ИЗЛАЗ** IZLAZ
OUT OF ORDER	**НЕ РАДИ** NE RADI

CLOSED	**ЗАТВОРЕНО** ZATVORENO
OPEN	**ОТВОРЕНО** OTVORENO
FOR WOMEN	**ЗА ЖЕНЕ** ZA ŽENE
FOR MEN	**ЗА МУШКАРЦЕ** ZA MUŠKARCE

Questions

Where?	**Где?** Gde?
Where to?	**Куда?** Kuda?
Where from?	**Одакле?** Odakle?
Why?	**Зашто?** Zašto?
For what reason?	**Из ког разлога?** Iz kog razloga?
When?	**Када?** Kada?
How long?	**Колико дуго?** Koliko dugo?
At what time?	**У колико сати?** U koliko sati?
How much?	**Колико?** Koliko?
Do you have ...?	**Имате ли ...?** Imate li ...?
Where is ...?	**Где се налази ...?** Gde se nalazi ...?
What time is it?	**Колико је сати?** Koliko je sati?
May I make a call?	**Смем ли да телефонирам?** Smem li da telefoniram?
Who's there?	**Ко је тамо?** Ko je tamo?
Can I smoke here?	**Да ли се овде пуши?** Da li se ovde puši?
May I ...?	**Смем ли ...?** Smem li ...?

Needs

I'd like …	**Волео /Волела/ бих …** Voleo /Volela/ bih …
I don't want …	**Не желим …** Ne želim …
I'm thirsty.	**Жедан /Жедна/ сам.** Žedan /Žedna/ sam
I want to sleep.	**Хоћу да спавам.** Hoću da spavam
I want …	**Хоћу …** Hoću …
to wash up	**да се освежим** da se osvežim
to brush my teeth	**да оперем зубе** da operem zube
to rest a while	**да се мало одморим** da se malo odmorim
to change my clothes	**да се пресвучем** da se presvučem
to go back to the hotel	**да се вратим у хотел** da se vratim u hotel
to buy …	**да купим …** da kupim …
to go to …	**да идем до …** da idem do …
to visit …	**да посетим …** da posetim …
to meet with …	**да се нађем са …** da se nađem sa …
to make a call	**да телефонирам** da telefoniram
I'm tired.	**Уморан /Уморна/ сам.** Umoran /Umorna/ sam
We are tired.	**Ми смо уморни.** Mi smo umorni
I'm cold.	**Хладно ми је.** Hladno mi je
I'm hot.	**Вруће ми је.** Vruće mi je
I'm OK.	**Добро сам.** Dobro sam

I need to make a call.

Треба да телефонирам.
Treba da telefoniram

I need to go to the restroom.

Морам до тоалета.
Moram do toaleta

I have to go.

Морам да идем.
Moram da idem

I have to go now.

Морам одмах да идем.
Moram odmah da idem

Asking for directions

Excuse me, ...	**Извините ...** Izvinite ...
Where is ...?	**Где се налази ...?** Gde se nalazi ...?
Which way is ...?	**Куда до ...?** Kuda do ...?
Could you help me, please?	**Можете ли ми, молим вас, помоћи?** Možete li mi, molim vas, pomoći?
I'm looking for ...	**Тражим ...** Tražim ...
I'm looking for the exit.	**Тражим излаз.** Tražim izlaz
I'm going to ...	**Идем до ...** Idem do ...
Am I going the right way to ...?	**Јесам ли на правом путу до ...?** Jesam li na pravom putu do ...?
Is it far?	**Да ли је далеко?** Da li je daleko?
Can I get there on foot?	**Могу ли до тамо пешке?** Mogu li do tamo peške?
Can you show me on the map?	**Можете ли да ми покажете на мапи?** Možete li da mi pokažete na mapi?
Show me where we are right now.	**Покажите ми где смо ми сада.** Pokažite mi gde smo mi sada
Here	**Овде** Ovde
There	**Тамо** Tamo
This way	**Овим путем** Ovim putem
Turn right.	**Скрените десно.** Skrenite desno
Turn left.	**Скрените лево.** Skrenite levo
first (second, third) turn	**прво (друго, треће) скретање** prvo (drugo, treće) skretanje

to the right	**десно** desno
to the left	**лево** levo
Go straight ahead.	**Идите само право.** Idite samo pravo

Signs

WELCOME!	**ДОБРОДОШЛИ!** DOBRODOŠLI!
ENTRANCE	**УЛАЗ** ULAZ
EXIT	**ИЗЛАЗ** IZLAZ
PUSH	**ГУРАЈ** GURAJ
PULL	**ВУЦИ** VUCI
OPEN	**ОТВОРЕНО** OTVORENO
CLOSED	**ЗАТВОРЕНО** ZATVORENO
FOR WOMEN	**ЗА ЖЕНЕ** ZA ŽENE
FOR MEN	**ЗА МУШКАРЦЕ** ZA MUŠKARCE
GENTLEMEN, GENTS (m)	**МУШКАРЦИ** MUŠKARCI
WOMEN (f)	**ЖЕНЕ** ŽENE
DISCOUNTS	**ПРОДАЈА** PRODAJA
SALE	**РАСПРОДАЈА** RASPRODAJA
FREE	**БЕСПЛАТНО** BESPLATNO
NEW!	**НОВО!** NOVO!
ATTENTION!	**ПАЖЊА!** PAŽNJA!
NO VACANCIES	**НЕМА СЛОБОДНИХ МЕСТА** NEMA SLOBODNIH MESTA
RESERVED	**РЕЗЕРВИСАНО** REZERVISANO
ADMINISTRATION	**АДМИНИСТРАЦИЈА** ADMINISTRACIJA
STAFF ONLY	**САМО ЗА ЗАПОСЛЕНЕ** SAMO ZA ZAPOSLENE

BEWARE OF THE DOG!	**ПАС УЈЕДА!** PAS UJEDA!
NO SMOKING!	**ЗАБРАЊЕНО ПУШЕЊЕ!** ZABRANJENO PUŠENJE!
DO NOT TOUCH!	**НЕ ПИПАЈ!** NE PIPAJ!
DANGEROUS	**ОПАСНО** OPASNO
DANGER	**ОПАСНОСТ** OPASNOST
HIGH VOLTAGE	**ВИСОК НАПОН** VISOK NAPON
NO SWIMMING!	**ЗАБРАЊЕНО ПЛИВАЊЕ!** ZABRANJENO PLIVANJE!

OUT OF ORDER	**НЕ РАДИ** NE RADI
FLAMMABLE	**ЗАПАЉИВО** ZAPALJIVO
FORBIDDEN	**ЗАБРАЊЕНО** ZABRANJENO
NO TRESPASSING!	**ЗАБРАЊЕН ПРОЛАЗ!** ZABRANJEN PROLAZ!
WET PAINT	**СВЕЖЕ ОКРЕЧЕНО** SVEŽE OKREČENO

CLOSED FOR RENOVATIONS	**ЗАТВОРЕНО ЗБОГ РЕНОВИРАЊА** ZATVORENO ZBOG RENOVIRANJA
WORKS AHEAD	**РАДОВИ НА ПУТУ** RADOVI NA PUTU
DETOUR	**ОБИЛАЗАК** OBILAZAK

Transportation. General phrases

plane	**авион** avion
train	**воз** voz
bus	**аутобус** autobus
ferry	**трајект** trajekt
taxi	**такси** taksi
car	**ауто** auto
schedule	**ред вожње** red vožnje
Where can I see the schedule?	**Где могу да видим ред вожње?** Gde mogu da vidim red vožnje?
workdays (weekdays)	**радни дани** radni dani
weekends	**викенди** vikendi
holidays	**празници** praznici
DEPARTURE	**ОДЛАЗАК** ODLAZAK
ARRIVAL	**ДОЛАЗАК** DOLAZAK
DELAYED	**КАСНИ** KASNI
CANCELLED	**ОТКАЗАН** OTKAZAN
next (train, etc.)	**следећи** sledeći
first	**први** prvi
last	**последњи** poslednji
When is the next ...?	**Када је следећи ...?** Kada je sledeći ...?
When is the first ...?	**Када је први ...?** Kada je prvi ...?

When is the last ...?	**Када је последњи ...?** Kada je poslednji ...?
transfer (change of trains, etc.)	**преседање** presedanje
to make a transfer	**имати преседање** imati presedanje
Do I need to make a transfer?	**Треба ли да пресседам?** Treba li da presedam?

Buying tickets

Where can I buy tickets?	**Где могу да купим карте?** Gde mogu da kupim karte?
ticket	**карта** karta
to buy a ticket	**купити карту** kupiti kartu
ticket price	**цена карте** cena karte
Where to?	**Куда?** Kuda?
To what station?	**До које станице?** Do koje stanice?
I need ...	**Треба ми ...** Treba mi ...
one ticket	**једна карта** jedna karta
two tickets	**две карте** dve karte
three tickets	**три карте** tri karte
one-way	**у једном правцу** u jednom pravcu
round-trip	**повратна** povratna
first class	**прва класа** prva klasa
second class	**друга класа** druga klasa
today	**данас** danas
tomorrow	**сутра** sutra
the day after tomorrow	**прекосутра** prekosutra
in the morning	**ујутру** ujutru
in the afternoon	**после подне** posle podne
in the evening	**увече** uveče

aisle seat

седиште до пролаза
sedište do prolaza

window seat

седиште поред прозора
sedište pored prozora

How much?

Колико?
Koliko?

Can I pay by credit card?

**Могу ли да платим
кредитном картицом?**
Mogu li da platim
kreditnom karticom?

Bus

bus	**Аутобус** Autobus
intercity bus	**међуградски аутобус** međugradski autobus
bus stop	**аутобуска станица** autobuska stanica
Where's the nearest bus stop?	**Где је најближа аутобуска станица?** Gde je najbliža autobuska stanica?
number (bus ~, etc.)	**број** broj
Which bus do I take to get to …?	**Којим аутобусом стижем до …?** Kojim autobusom stižem do …?
Does this bus go to …?	**Да ли овај аутобус иде до …?** Da li ovaj autobus ide do …?
How frequent are the buses?	**Колико често иду аутобуси?** Koliko često idu autobusi?
every 15 minutes	**сваких 15 минута** svakih 15 minuta
every half hour	**сваких пола сата** svakih pola sata
every hour	**сваки сат** svaki sat
several times a day	**неколико пута дневно** nekoliko puta dnevno
… times a day	**… пута дневно** … puta dnevno
schedule	**ред вожње** red vožnje
Where can I see the schedule?	**Где могу да видим ред вожње?** Gde mogu da vidim red vožnje?
When is the next bus?	**Када је следећи аутобус?** Kada je sledeći autobus?
When is the first bus?	**Када је први аутобус?** Kada je prvi autobus?
When is the last bus?	**Када је последњи аутобус?** Kada je poslednji autobus?
stop	**станица** stanica
next stop	**следећа станица** sledeća stanica

last stop (terminus)

последња станица
poslednja stanica

Stop here, please.

Станите овде, молим вас.
Stanite ovde, molim vas

Excuse me, this is my stop.

Извините, ово је моја станица.
Izvinite, ovo je moja stanica

Train

train	**воз** voz
suburban train	**приградски воз** prigradski voz
long-distance train	**међуградски воз** međugradski voz
train station	**железничка станица** železnička stanica
Excuse me, where is the exit to the platform?	**Извините, где је излаз до перона?** Izvinite, gde je izlaz do perona?
Does this train go to ...?	**Да ли овај воз иде до ...?** Da li ovaj voz ide do ...?
next train	**следећи воз** sledeći voz
When is the next train?	**Када полази следећи воз?** Kada polazi sledeći voz?
Where can I see the schedule?	**Где могу да видим ред вожње?** Gde mogu da vidim red vožnje?
From which platform?	**Са ког перона?** Sa kog perona?
When does the train arrive in ...?	**Када воз стиже у ...?** Kada voz stiže u ...?
Please help me.	**Молим вас, помозите ми.** Molim vas, pomozite mi
I'm looking for my seat.	**Тражим своје место.** Tražim svoje mesto
We're looking for our seats.	**Ми тражимо своја места.** Mi tražimo svoja mesta
My seat is taken.	**Моје место је заузето.** Moje mesto je zauzeto
Our seats are taken.	**Наша места су заузета.** Naša mesta su zauzeta
I'm sorry but this is my seat.	**Извините, али ово је моје место.** Izvinite, ali ovo je moje mesto
Is this seat taken?	**Да ли је ово место заузето?** Da li je ovo mesto zauzeto?
May I sit here?	**Могу ли овде да седнем?** Mogu li ovde da sednem?

On the train. Dialogue (No ticket)

Ticket, please.
Карту, молим вас.
Kartu, molim vas

I don't have a ticket.
Немам карту.
Nemam kartu

I lost my ticket.
Изгубио сам карту.
Izgubio sam kartu

I forgot my ticket at home.
Заборавио сам карту код куће.
Zaboravio sam kartu kod kuće

You can buy a ticket from me.
Од мене можете купити карту.
Od mene možete kupiti kartu

You will also have to pay a fine.
Такође ћете морати да платите казну.
Takođe ćete morati da platite kaznu

Okay.
У реду.
U redu

Where are you going?
Где идете?
Gde idete?

I'm going to ...
Идем до ...
Idem do ...

How much? I don't understand.
Колико? Не разумем.
Koliko? Ne razumem

Write it down, please.
Напишите, молим вас.
Napišite, molim vas

Okay. Can I pay with a credit card?
У реду. Да ли могу да платим кредитном картицом?
U redu. Da li mogu da platim kreditnom karticom?

Yes, you can.
Да, можете.
Da, možete

Here's your receipt.
Изволите рачун.
Izvolite račun

Sorry about the fine.
Извините због казне.
Izvinite zbog kazne

That's okay. It was my fault.
У реду је. Моја грешка.
U redu je. Moja greška

Enjoy your trip.
Уживајте у путовању.
Uživajte u putovanju

Taxi

taxi	**такси** taksi
taxi driver	**таксиста** taksista
to catch a taxi	**ухватити такси** uhvatiti taksi
taxi stand	**такси станица** taksi stanica
Where can I get a taxi?	**Где могу да нађем такси?** Gde mogu da nađem taksi?

to call a taxi	**позвати такси** pozvati taksi
I need a taxi.	**Треба ми такси.** Treba mi taksi
Right now.	**Одмах.** Odmah
What is your address (location)?	**Која је ваша адреса?** Koja je vaša adresa?
My address is ...	**Моја адреса је ...** Moja adresa je ...
Your destination?	**Докле идете?** Dokle idete?

Excuse me, ...	**Извините ...** Izvinite ...
Are you available?	**Да ли сте слободни?** Da li ste slobodni?
How much is it to get to ...?	**Колико кошта до ...?** Koliko košta do ...?
Do you know where it is?	**Да ли знате где је?** Da li znate gde je?
Airport, please.	**Аеродром, молим.** Aerodrom, molim
Stop here, please.	**Станите овде, молим вас.** Stanite ovde, molim vas
It's not here.	**Није овде.** Nije ovde
This is the wrong address.	**Ово је погрешна адреса.** Ovo je pogrešna adresa
Turn left.	**скрените лево** skrenite levo
Turn right.	**скрените десно** skrenite desno

How much do I owe you?	**Колико вам дугујем?** Koliko vam dugujem?
I'd like a receipt, please.	**Рачун, молим.** Račun, molim
Keep the change.	**Задржите кусур.** Zadržite kusur

Would you please wait for me?	**Да ли бисте ме сачекали, молим вас?** Da li biste me sačekali, molim vas?
five minutes	**пет минута** pet minuta
ten minutes	**десет минута** deset minuta
fifteen minutes	**петнаест минута** petnaest minuta
twenty minutes	**двадесет минута** dvadeset minuta
half an hour	**пола сата** pola sata

Hotel

Hello.	**Добар дан.** Dobar dan
My name is ...	**Ја се зовем ...** Ja se zovem ...
I have a reservation.	**Имам резервацију.** Imam rezervaciju
I need ...	**Треба ми ...** Treba mi ...
a single room	**једнокреветна соба** jednokrevetna soba
a double room	**двокреветна соба** dvokrevetna soba
How much is that?	**Колико је то?** Koliko je to?
That's a bit expensive.	**То је мало скупо.** To je malo skupo
Do you have anything else?	**Да ли имате неку другу могућност?** Da li imate neku drugu mogućnost?
I'll take it.	**Узећу то.** Uzeću to
I'll pay in cash.	**Платићу готовином.** Platiću gotovinom
I've got a problem.	**Имам проблем.** Imam problem
My ... is broken.	**Мој ... је сломљен** **/Моја... је сломљена/.** Moj ... je slomljen /slomljena/
My ... is out of order.	**Мој /Моја/ ... не ради.** Moj /Moja/ ... ne radi
TV	**телевизор (м)** televizor
air conditioner	**клима уређај (м)** klima uređaj
tap	**славина (ж)** slavina
shower	**туш (м)** tuš
sink	**лавабо (м)** lavabo

safe	**сеф (м)** sef
door lock	**брава (ж)** brava
electrical outlet	**електрична утичница (ж)** električna utičnica
hairdryer	**фен (м)** fen
I don't have …	**Немам …** Nemam …
water	**воде** vode
light	**светла** svetla
electricity	**струје** struje
Can you give me …?	**Можете ли ми дати …?** Možete li mi dati …?
a towel	**пешкир** peškir
a blanket	**ћебе** ćebe
slippers	**папуче** papuče
a robe	**баде-мантил** bade-mantil
shampoo	**мало шампона** malo šampona
soap	**мало сапуна** malo sapuna
I'd like to change rooms.	**Хоћу да заменим собу.** Hoću da zamenim sobu
I can't find my key.	**Не могу да нађем свој кључ.** Ne mogu da nađem svoj ključ
Could you open my room, please?	**Можете ли ми отворити собу, молим вас?** Možete li mi otvoriti sobu, molim vas?
Who's there?	**Ко је тамо?** Ko je tamo?
Come in!	**Уђите!** Uđite!
Just a minute!	**Само тренутак!** Samo trenutak!
Not right now, please.	**Не сада, молим вас.** Ne sada, molim vas
Come to my room, please.	**Дођите у моју собу, молим вас.** Dođite u moju sobu, molim vas

I'd like to order food service.	**Хтео бих да поручим храну.** Hteo bih da poručim hranu
My room number is ...	**Број моје собе је ...** Broj moje sobe je ...

I'm leaving ...	**Одлазим ...** Odlazim ...
We're leaving ...	**Ми одлазимо ...** Mi odlazimo ...
right now	**одмах** odmah
this afternoon	**овог поподнева** ovog popodneva
tonight	**вечерас** večeras
tomorrow	**сутра** sutra
tomorrow morning	**сутра ујутру** sutra ujutru
tomorrow evening	**сутра увече** sutra uveče
the day after tomorrow	**прекосутра** prekosutra

I'd like to pay.	**Хтео бих да платим.** Hteo bih da platim
Everything was wonderful.	**Све је било дивно.** Sve je bilo divno
Where can I get a taxi?	**Где могу да нађем такси?** Gde mogu da nađem taksi?
Would you call a taxi for me, please?	**Да ли бисте ми позвали такси, молим вас?** Da li biste mi pozvali taksi, molim vas?

Restaurant

Can I look at the menu, please?	**Могу ли да погледам мени, молим вас?** Mogu li da pogledam meni, molim vas?
Table for one.	**Сто за једног.** Sto za jednog
There are two (three, four) of us.	**Има нас двоје (троје, четворо).** Ima nas dvoje (troje, četvoro)
Smoking	**За пушаче** Za pušače
No smoking	**За непушаче** Za nepušače
Excuse me! (addressing a waiter)	**Конобар!** Konobar!
menu	**мени** meni
wine list	**винска карта** vinska karta
The menu, please.	**Мени, молим вас.** Meni, molim vas
Are you ready to order?	**Да ли сте спремни да наручите?** Da li ste spremni da naručite?
What will you have?	**Шта бисте хтели?** Šta biste hteli?
I'll have ...	**Ја ћу ...** Ja ću ...
I'm a vegetarian.	**Ја сам вегетеријанац /вегетаријанка/.** Ja sam vegeterijanac /vegetarijanka/
meat	**месо** meso
fish	**рибу** ribu
vegetables	**поврће** povrće
Do you have vegetarian dishes?	**Имате ли вегетеријанска јела?** Imate li vegeterijanska jela?
I don't eat pork.	**Не једем свињетину.** Ne jedem svinjetinu

He /she/ doesn't eat meat.	**Он /Она/ не једе месо.** On /Ona/ ne jede meso
I am allergic to …	**Алергичан /Алергична/ сам на …** Alergičan /Alergična/ sam na …

Would you please bring me …	**Да ли бисте ми,** **молим вас, донели …** Da li biste mi, molim vas, doneli …
salt | pepper | sugar	**со | бибер | шећер** so | biber | šećer
coffee | tea | dessert	**кафу | чај | дезерт** kafu | čaj | dezert
water | sparkling | plain	**воду | газирану | негазирану** vodu | gaziranu | negaziranu
a spoon | fork | knife	**кашику | виљушку | нож** kašiku | viljušku | nož
a plate | napkin	**тањир | салвету** tanjir | salvetu

Enjoy your meal!	**Пријатно!** Prijatno!
One more, please.	**Још једно, молим.** Još jedno, molim
It was very delicious.	**Било је изврсно.** Bilo je izvrsno

check | change | tip	**рачун | кусур | бакшиш** račun | kusur | bakšiš
Check, please. (Could I have the check, please?)	**Рачун, молим.** Račun, molim
Can I pay by credit card?	**Могу ли да платим** **кредитном картицом?** Mogu li da platim kreditnom karticom?
I'm sorry, there's a mistake here.	**Извините, овде је грешка.** Izvinite, ovde je greška

Shopping

Can I help you?	**Могу ли да вам помогнем?** Mogu li da vam pomognem?
Do you have …?	**Имате ли …?** Imate li …?
I'm looking for …	**Тражим …** Tražim …
I need …	**Треба ми …** Treba mi …
I'm just looking.	**Само гледам.** Samo gledam
We're just looking.	**Само гледамо.** Samo gledamo
I'll come back later.	**Вратићу се касније.** Vratiću se kasnije
We'll come back later.	**Вратићемо се касније.** Vratićemo se kasnije
discounts | sale	**попусти | распродаја** popusti | rasprodaja
Would you please show me …	**Да ли бисте ми, молим вас, показали …** Da li biste mi, molim vas, pokazali …
Would you please give me …	**Да ли бисте ми, молим вас, дали …** Da li biste mi, molim vas, dali …
Can I try it on?	**Могу ли да пробам?** Mogu li da probam?
Excuse me, where's the fitting room?	**Извините, где је кабина за пресвлачење?** Izvinite, gde je kabina za presvlačenje?
Which color would you like?	**Коју боју бисте хтели?** Koju boju biste hteli?
size | length	**величина | дужина** veličina | dužina
How does it fit?	**Како ми стоји?** Kako mi stoji?
How much is it?	**Колико кошта?** Koliko košta?
That's too expensive.	**То је прескупо.** To je preskupo

I'll take it.	**Узећу то.** Uzeću to
Excuse me, where do I pay?	**Извините, где се плаћа?** Izvinite, gde se plaća?
Will you pay in cash or credit card?	**Плаћате ли готовином или кредитном картицом?** Plaćate li gotovinom ili kreditnom karticom?
In cash	with credit card	**Готовином	кредитном картицом** Gotovinom	kreditnom karticom

Do you want the receipt?	**Желите ли рачун?** Želite li račun?
Yes, please.	**Да, молим.** Da, molim
No, it's OK.	**Не, у реду је.** Ne, u redu je
Thank you. Have a nice day!	**Хвала. Пријатно!** Hvala. Prijatno!

In town

| Excuse me, please. | **Извините, молим вас …**
Izvinite, molim vas … |
| I'm looking for … | **Тражим …**
Tražim … |

the subway	**метро** metro
my hotel	**свој хотел** svoj hotel
the movie theater	**биоскоп** bioskop
a taxi stand	**такси станицу** taksi stanicu

an ATM	**банкомат** bankomat
a foreign exchange office	**мењачницу** menjačnicu
an internet café	**интернет кафе** internet kafe
… street	**улицу …** ulicu …
this place	**ово место** ovo mesto

| Do you know where … is? | **Знате ли где је …?**
Znate li gde je …? |
| Which street is this? | **Која је ово улица?**
Koja je ovo ulica? |

Show me where we are right now.	**Покажите ми где смо ми сада.** Pokažite mi gde smo mi sada
Can I get there on foot?	**Могу ли до тамо пешке?** Mogu li do tamo peške?
Do you have a map of the city?	**Имате ли мапу града?** Imate li mapu grada?

How much is a ticket to get in?	**Колико кошта улазница?** Koliko košta ulaznica?
Can I take pictures here?	**Могу ли овде да се сликам?** Mogu li ovde da se slikam?
Are you open?	**Да ли радите?** Da li radite?

When do you open?

Када отварате?
Kada otvarate?

When do you close?

Када затварате?
Kada zatvarate?

Money

money	**новац** novac
cash	**готовина** gotovina
paper money	**папирни новац** papirni novac
loose change	**кусур, ситниш** kusur, sitniš
check | change | tip	**рачун | кусур | бакшиш** račun | kusur | bakšiš
credit card	**кредитна картица** kreditna kartica
wallet	**новчаник** novčanik
to buy	**купити** kupiti
to pay	**платити** platiti
fine	**казна** kazna
free	**бесплатно** besplatno
Where can I buy ...?	**Где могу да купим ...?** Gde mogu da kupim ...?
Is the bank open now?	**Да ли је банка отворена сада?** Da li je banka otvorena sada?
When does it open?	**Када се отвара?** Kada se otvara?
When does it close?	**Када се затвара?** Kada se zatvara?
How much?	**Колико?** Koliko?
How much is this?	**Колико ово кошта?** Koliko ovo košta?
That's too expensive.	**То је прескупо.** To je preskupo
Excuse me, where do I pay?	**Извините, где се плаћа?** Izvinite, gde se plaća?
Check, please.	**Рачун, молим.** Račun, molim

Can I pay by credit card?	**Могу ли да платим кредитном картицом?** Mogu li da platim kreditnom karticom?
Is there an ATM here?	**Да ли овде негде има банкомат?** Da li ovde negde ima bankomat?
I'm looking for an ATM.	**Тражим банкомат.** Tražim bankomat

I'm looking for a foreign exchange office.	**Тражим мењачницу.** Tražim menjačnicu
I'd like to change ...	**Хтео бих да заменим ...** Hteo bih da zamenim ...
What is the exchange rate?	**Колики је курс?** Koliki je kurs?
Do you need my passport?	**Да ли вам треба мој пасош?** Da li vam treba moj pasoš?

Time

What time is it?	**Колико је сати?** Koliko je sati?
When?	**Када?** Kada?
At what time?	**У колико сати?** U koliko sati?
now | later | after …	**сада | касније | после …** sada | kasnije | posle …
one o'clock	**један сат** jedan sat
one fifteen	**један и петнаест** jedan i petnaest
one thirty	**пола два** pola dva
one forty-five	**петнаест до два** petnaest do dva
one | two | three	**један | два | три** jedan | dva | tri
four | five | six	**четири | пет | шест** četiri | pet | šest
seven | eight | nine	**седам | осам | девет** sedam | osam | devet
ten | eleven | twelve	**десет | једанаест | дванаест** deset | jedanaest | dvanaest
in …	**за …** za …
five minutes	**пет минута** pet minuta
ten minutes	**десет минута** deset minuta
fifteen minutes	**петнаест минута** petnaest minuta
twenty minutes	**двадесет минута** dvadeset minuta
half an hour	**пола сата** pola sata
an hour	**сат времена** sat vremena

in the morning	**ујутру** ujutru
early in the morning	**рано ујутру** rano ujutru
this morning	**овог јутра** ovog jutra
tomorrow morning	**сутра ујутру** sutra ujutru
in the middle of the day	**за време ручка** za vreme ručka
in the afternoon	**после подне** posle podne
in the evening	**увече** uveče
tonight	**вечерас** večeras
at night	**ноћу** noću
yesterday	**јуче** juče
today	**данас** danas
tomorrow	**сутра** sutra
the day after tomorrow	**прекосутра** prekosutra
What day is it today?	**Који је данас дан?** Koji je danas dan?
It's …	**Данас је …** Danas je …
Monday	**Понедељак** Ponedeljak
Tuesday	**Уторак** Utorak
Wednesday	**Среда** Sreda
Thursday	**Четвртак** Četvrtak
Friday	**Петак** Petak
Saturday	**Субота** Subota
Sunday	**Недеља** Nedelja

Greetings. Introductions

Hello.	**Здраво.** Zdravo
Pleased to meet you.	**Драго ми је што смо се упознали.** Drago mi je što smo se upoznali
Me too.	**И мени.** I meni
I'd like you to meet …	**Хтео бих да упознаш …** Hteo bih da upoznaš …
Nice to meet you.	**Драго ми је што смо се упознали.** Drago mi je što smo se upoznali

How are you?	**Како сте?** Kako ste?
My name is …	**Ја се зовем …** Ja se zovem …
His name is …	**Он се зове …** On se zove …
Her name is …	**Она се зове …** Ona se zove …
What's your name?	**Како се ви зовете?** Kako se vi zovete?
What's his name?	**Како се он зове?** Kako se on zove?
What's her name?	**Како се она зове?** Kako se ona zove?

What's your last name?	**Како се презивате?** Kako se prezivate?
You can call me …	**Можете ме звати …** Možete me zvati …
Where are you from?	**Одакле сте?** Odakle ste?
I'm from …	**Ја сам из …** Ja sam iz …
What do you do for a living?	**Чиме се бавите?** Čime se bavite?

Who is this?	**Ко је ово?** Ko je ovo?
Who is he?	**Ко је он?** Ko je on?
Who is she?	**Ко је она?** Ko je ona?

Who are they?	**Ко су они?** Ko su oni?
This is ...	**Ово је ...** Ovo je ...
my friend (masc.)	**мој пријатељ** moj prijatelj
my friend (fem.)	**моја пријатељица** moja prijateljica
my husband	**мој муж** moj muž
my wife	**моја жена** moja žena
my father	**мој отац** moj otac
my mother	**моја мајка** moja majka
my brother	**мој брат** moj brat
my sister	**моја сестра** moja sestra
my son	**мој син** moj sin
my daughter	**моја ћерка** moja ćerka
This is our son.	**Ово је наш син.** Ovo je naš sin
This is our daughter.	**Ово је наша ћерка.** Ovo je naša ćerka
These are my children.	**Ово су моја деца.** Ovo su moja deca
These are our children.	**Ово су наша деца.** Ovo su naša deca

Farewells

Good bye!	**Довиђења!** Doviđenja!
Bye! (inform.)	**Ћао!** Ćao!
See you tomorrow.	**Видимо се сутра.** Vidimo se sutra
See you soon.	**Видимо се ускоро.** Vidimo se uskoro
See you at seven.	**Видимо се у седам.** Vidimo se u sedam
Have fun!	**Лепо се проведите!** Lepo se provedite!
Talk to you later.	**Чујемо се касније.** Čujemo se kasnije
Have a nice weekend.	**Леп викенд.** Lep vikend
Good night.	**Лаку ноћ.** Laku noć
It's time for me to go.	**Време је да кренем.** Vreme je da krenem
I have to go.	**Морам да кренем.** Moram da krenem
I will be right back.	**Одмах се враћам.** Odmah se vraćam
It's late.	**Касно је.** Kasno je
I have to get up early.	**Морам рано да устанем.** Moram rano da ustanem
I'm leaving tomorrow.	**Одлазим сутра.** Odlazim sutra
We're leaving tomorrow.	**Одлазимо сутра.** Odlazimo sutra
Have a nice trip!	**Лепо се проведите на путу!** Lepo se provedite na putu!
It was nice meeting you.	**Драго ми је што смо се упознали.** Drago mi je što smo se upoznali
It was nice talking to you.	**Драго ми је што смо поразговарали.** Drago mi je što smo porazgovarali
Thanks for everything.	**Хвала на свему.** Hvala na svemu

I had a very good time.	**Лепо сам се провео /провела/.** Lepo sam se proveo /provela/
We had a very good time.	**Лепо смо се провели.** Lepo smo se proveli
It was really great.	**Било је супер.** Bilo je super
I'm going to miss you.	**Недостајаћете ми.** Nedostajaćete mi
We're going to miss you.	**Недостајаћете нам.** Nedostajaćete nam
Good luck!	**Срећно!** Srećno!
Say hi to …	**Поздравите …** Pozdravite …

Foreign language

I don't understand.	**Не разумем.** Ne razumem
Write it down, please.	**Можете ли то записати?** Možete li to zapisati?
Do you speak ...?	**Да ли говорите ...?** Da li govorite ...?
I speak a little bit of ...	**Помало говорим ...** Pomalo govorim ...
English	**Енглески** Engleski
Turkish	**Турски** Turski
Arabic	**Арапски** Arapski
French	**Француски** Francuski
German	**Немачки** Nemački
Italian	**Италијански** Italijanski
Spanish	**Шпански** Španski
Portuguese	**Португалски** Portugalski
Chinese	**Кинески** Kineski
Japanese	**Јапански** Japanski
Can you repeat that, please.	**Можете ли то да поновите, молим вас.** Možete li to da ponovite, molim vas
I understand.	**Разумем.** Razumem
I don't understand.	**Не разумем.** Ne razumem
Please speak more slowly.	**Молим вас, говорите спорије.** Molim vas, govorite sporije

Is that correct? (Am I saying it right?)   **Јел' тако?**
Jel' tako?

What is this? (What does this mean?)   **Шта је ово?**
Šta je ovo?

Apologies

Excuse me, please.	**Извините, молим вас.** Izvinite, molim vas
I'm sorry.	**Извините.** Izvinite
I'm really sorry.	**Јако ми је жао.** Jako mi je žao
Sorry, it's my fault.	**Извините, ја сам крив.** Izvinite, ja sam kriv
My mistake.	**Моја грешка.** Moja greška
May I ...?	**Смем ли ...?** Smem li ...?
Do you mind if I ...?	**Да ли би вам сметало да ...?** Da li bi vam smetalo da ...?
It's OK.	**OK је.** OK je
It's all right.	**У реду је.** U redu je
Don't worry about it.	**Не брините.** Ne brinite

Agreement

Yes.	**Да.** Da
Yes, sure.	**Да, свакако.** Da, svakako
OK (Good!)	**Добро, важи!** Dobro, važi!
Very well.	**Врло добро.** Vrlo dobro
Certainly!	**Свакако!** Svakako!
I agree.	**Слажем се.** Slažem se
That's correct.	**Тако је.** Tako je
That's right.	**То је тачно.** To je tačno
You're right.	**Ви сте у праву.** Vi ste u pravu
I don't mind.	**Не смета ми.** Ne smeta mi
Absolutely right.	**Потпуно тачно.** Potpuno tačno
It's possible.	**Могуће је.** Moguće je
That's a good idea.	**То је добра идеја.** To je dobra ideja
I can't say no.	**Не могу да одбијем.** Ne mogu da odbijem
I'd be happy to.	**Биће ми задовољство.** Biće mi zadovoljstvo
With pleasure.	**Са задовољством.** Sa zadovoljstvom

Refusal. Expressing doubt

No.	**Не.** Ne
Certainly not.	**Нипошто.** Nipošto
I don't agree.	**Не слажем се.** Ne slažem se
I don't think so.	**Не мислим тако.** Ne mislim tako
It's not true.	**Није истина.** Nije istina
You are wrong.	**Грешите.** Grešite
I think you are wrong.	**Мислим да грешите.** Mislim da grešite
I'm not sure.	**Нисам сигуран /сигурна/.** Nisam siguran /sigurna/
It's impossible.	**Немогуће.** Nemoguće
Nothing of the kind (sort)!	**Нема шансе!** Nema šanse!
The exact opposite.	**Потпуно супротно.** Potpuno suprotno
I'm against it.	**Ја сам против тога.** Ja sam protiv toga
I don't care.	**Баш ме брига.** Baš me briga
I have no idea.	**Немам појма.** Nemam pojma
I doubt it.	**Не мислим тако.** Ne mislim tako
Sorry, I can't.	**Жао ми је, не могу.** Žao mi je, ne mogu
Sorry, I don't want to.	**Жао ми је, не желим.** Žao mi je, ne želim
Thank you, but I don't need this.	**Хвала, али то ми није потребно.** Hvala, ali to mi nije potrebno
It's getting late.	**Већ је касно.** Već je kasno

I have to get up early.

Морам рано да устанем.
Moram rano da ustanem

I don't feel well.

Не осећам се добро.
Ne osećam se dobro

Expressing gratitude

Thank you. **Хвала вам.**
Hvala vam

Thank you very much. **Много вам хвала.**
Mnogo vam hvala

I really appreciate it. **Заиста то ценим.**
Zaista to cenim

I'm really grateful to you. **Заиста сам вам захвалан /захвална/.**
Zaista sam vam zahvalan /zahvalna/

We are really grateful to you. **Заиста смо вам захвални.**
Zaista smo vam zahvalni

Thank you for your time. **Хвала вам на времену.**
Hvala vam na vremenu

Thanks for everything. **Хвала на свему.**
Hvala na svemu

Thank you for ... **Хвала вам на ...**
Hvala vam na ...

your help **вашој помоћи**
vašoj pomoći

a nice time **на лепом проводу**
na lepom provodu

a wonderful meal **лепом оброку**
lepom obroku

a pleasant evening **лепој вечери**
lepoj večeri

a wonderful day **дивном дану**
divnom danu

an amazing journey **сјајном путовању**
sjajnom putovanju

Don't mention it. **Није то ништа.**
Nije to ništa

You are welcome. **Нема на чему.**
Nema na čemu

Any time. **У свако доба.**
U svako doba

My pleasure. **Било ми је задовољство.**
Bilo mi je zadovoljstvo

Forget it. **Заборавите на то.**
Zaboravite na to

Don't worry about it. **Не брините за то.**
Ne brinite za to

Congratulations. Best wishes

Congratulations!	**Честитам!** Čestitam!
Happy birthday!	**Срећан рођендан!** Srećan rođendan!
Merry Christmas!	**Срећан Божић!** Srećan Božić!
Happy New Year!	**Срећна Нова година!** Srećna Nova godina!
Happy Easter!	**Срећан Ускрс!** Srećan Uskrs!
Happy Hanukkah!	**Срећна Ханука!** Srećna Hanuka!
I'd like to propose a toast.	**Хтео бих да наздравим.** Hteo bih da nazdravim
Cheers!	**Живели!** Živeli!
Let's drink to …!	**Попијмо у име …!** Popijmo u ime …!
To our success!	**За наш успех!** Za naš uspeh!
To your success!	**За ваш успех!** Za vaš uspeh!
Good luck!	**Срећно!** Srećno!
Have a nice day!	**Пријатан дан!** Prijatan dan!
Have a good holiday!	**Уживајте на одмору!** Uživajte na odmoru!
Have a safe journey!	**Срећан пут!** Srećan put!
I hope you get better soon!	**Надам се да ћете се ускоро опоравити!** Nadam se da ćete se uskoro oporaviti!

Socializing

Why are you sad?	**Зашто си тужна?** Zašto si tužna?
Smile! Cheer up!	**Насмеши се! Разведри се!** Nasmeši se! Razvedri se!
Are you free tonight?	**Да ли си слободна вечерас?** Da li si slobodna večeras?
May I offer you a drink?	**Могу ли вам понудити пиће?** Mogu li vam ponuditi piće?
Would you like to dance?	**Да ли сте за плес?** Da li ste za ples?
Let's go to the movies.	**Хајдемо у биоскоп.** Hajdemo u bioskop
May I invite you to ...?	**Могу ли вас позвати у ...?** Mogu li vas pozvati u ...?
a restaurant	**ресторан** restoran
the movies	**биоскоп** bioskop
the theater	**позориште** pozorište
go for a walk	**у шетњу** u šetnju
At what time?	**У колико сати?** U koliko sati?
tonight	**вечерас** večeras
at six	**у шест** u šest
at seven	**у седам** u sedam
at eight	**у осам** u osam
at nine	**у девет** u devet
Do you like it here?	**Да ли ти се допада овде?** Da li ti se dopada ovde?
Are you here with someone?	**Да ли си овде са неким?** Da li si ovde sa nekim?
I'm with my friend.	**Са пријатељем /пријатељицом/.** Sa prijateljem /prijateljicom/

I'm with my friends.	Са пријатељима.
	Sa prijateljima
No, I'm alone.	Не, сâм сам. /Не, сама сам/.
	Ne, sâm sam. /Ne, sama sam/

Do you have a boyfriend?	Да ли имаш дечка?
	Da li imaš dečka?
I have a boyfriend.	Имам дечка.
	Imam dečka
Do you have a girlfriend?	Да ли имаш девојку?
	Da li imaš devojku?
I have a girlfriend.	Имам девојку.
	Imam devojku

Can I see you again?	Могу ли опет да те видим?
	Mogu li opet da te vidim?
Can I call you?	Могу ли да те позовем?
	Mogu li da te pozovem?
Call me. (Give me a call.)	Позови ме.
	Pozovi me
What's your number?	Који ти је број телефона?
	Koji ti je broj telefona?
I miss you.	Недостајеш ми.
	Nedostaješ mi

You have a beautiful name.	Имате лепо име.
	Imate lepo ime
I love you.	Волим те.
	Volim te
Will you marry me?	Удај се за мене.
	Udaj se za mene
You're kidding!	Шалите се!
	Šalite se!
I'm just kidding.	Само се шалим.
	Samo se šalim

Are you serious?	Да ли сте озбиљни?
	Da li ste ozbiljni?
I'm serious.	Озбиљан сам.
	Ozbiljan sam
Really?!	Стварно?!
	Stvarno?!
It's unbelievable!	То је невероватно!
	To je neverovatno!
I don't believe you.	Не верујем вам.
	Ne verujem vam

I can't.	Не могу.
	Ne mogu
I don't know.	Не знам.
	Ne znam

I don't understand you.

Не разумем те.
Ne razumem te

Please go away.

Молим вас, одлазите.
Molim vas, odlazite

Leave me alone!

Оставите ме на миру!
Ostavite me na miru!

I can't stand him.

Не могу да га поднесем.
Ne mogu da ga podnesem

You are disgusting!

Одвратни сте!
Odvratni ste!

I'll call the police!

Зваћу полицију!
Zvaću policiju!

Sharing impressions. Emotions

I like it.	**Свиђа ми се то.** Sviđa mi se to
Very nice.	**Баш лепо.** Baš lepo
That's great!	**То је супер!** To je super!
It's not bad.	**Није лоше.** Nije loše
I don't like it.	**Не свиђа ми се.** Ne sviđa mi se
It's not good.	**Није добро.** Nije dobro
It's bad.	**Лоше је.** Loše je
It's very bad.	**Много је лоше.** Mnogo je loše
It's disgusting.	**Грозно је.** Grozno je
I'm happy.	**Срећан /Срећна/ сам.** Srećan /Srećna/ sam
I'm content.	**Задовољан /Задовољна/ сам.** Zadovoljan /Zadovoljna/ sam
I'm in love.	**Заљубљен /Заљубљена/ сам.** Zaljubljen /Zaljubljena/ sam
I'm calm.	**Миран /Мирна/ сам.** Miran /Mirna/ sam
I'm bored.	**Досадно ми је.** Dosadno mi je
I'm tired.	**Уморан /Уморна/ сам.** Umoran /Umorna/ sam
I'm sad.	**Тужан /Тужна/ сам.** Tužan /Tužna/ sam
I'm frightened.	**Уплашен /Уплашена/ сам.** Uplašen /Uplašena/ sam
I'm angry.	**Љут /Љута/ сам.** Ljut /Ljuta/ sam
I'm worried.	**Забринут /Забринута/ сам.** Zabrinut /Zabrinuta/ sam
I'm nervous.	**Нервозан /Нервозна/ сам.** Nervozan /Nervozna/ sam

I'm jealous. (envious)

Љубоморан /Љубоморна/ сам.
Ljubomoran /Ljubomorna/ sam

I'm surprised.

Изненађен /Изненађена/ сам.
Iznenađen /Iznenađena/ sam

I'm perplexed.

Збуњен /Збуњена/ сам.
Zbunjen /Zbunjena/ sam

Problems. Accidents

I've got a problem.	**Имам проблем.** Imam problem
We've got a problem.	**Имамо проблем.** Imamo problem
I'm lost.	**Изгубио /Изгубила/ сам се.** Izgubio /Izgubila/ sam se
I missed the last bus (train).	**Пропустио /пропустила/ сам последњи аутобус (воз).** Propustio /propustila/ sam poslednji autobus (voz)
I don't have any money left.	**Немам више новца.** Nemam više novca

I've lost my …	**Изгубио /Изгубила/ сам …** Izgubio /Izgubila/ sam …
Someone stole my …	**Неко ми је украо …** Neko mi je ukrao …

passport	**пасош** pasoš
wallet	**новчаник** novčanik
papers	**папире** papire
ticket	**карту** kartu

money	**новац** novac
handbag	**ташну** tašnu
camera	**фото-апарат** foto-aparat
laptop	**лаптоп** laptop
tablet computer	**таблет рачунар** tablet računar
mobile phone	**мобилни телефон** mobilni telefon

Help me!	**Помозите ми!** Pomozite mi!
What's happened?	**Шта се десило?** Šta se desilo?

fire	**пожар**
	požar
shooting	**пуцњава**
	pucnjava
murder	**убиство**
	ubistvo
explosion	**експлозија**
	eksplozija
fight	**туча**
	tuča

Call the police!	**Позовите полицију!**
	Pozovite policiju!
Please hurry up!	**Молим вас, пожурите!**
	Molim vas, požurite!
I'm looking for the police station.	**Тражим полицијску станицу.**
	Tražim policijsku stanicu
I need to make a call.	**Морам да телефонирам.**
	Moram da telefoniram
May I use your phone?	**Могу ли да се послужим вашим телефоном?**
	Mogu li da se poslužim vašim telefonom?

I've been ...	**Неко ме је ...**
	Neko me je ...
mugged	**покрао**
	pokrao
robbed	**опљачкао**
	opljačkao
raped	**силовао**
	silovao
attacked (beaten up)	**напао**
	napao

Are you all right?	**Да ли сте добро?**
	Da li ste dobro?
Did you see who it was?	**Да ли сте видели ко је то био?**
	Da li ste videli ko je to bio?
Would you be able to recognize the person?	**Да ли бисте могли да препознате ту особу?**
	Da li biste mogli da prepoznate tu osobu?
Are you sure?	**Да ли сте сигурни?**
	Da li ste sigurni?

Please calm down.	**Молим вас, смирите се.**
	Molim vas, smirite se
Take it easy!	**Само полако!**
	Samo polako!
Don't worry!	**Не бpadните!**
	Ne brinite!

Everything will be fine.	**Све ће бити у реду.** Sve će biti u redu
Everything's all right.	**Све је у реду.** Sve je u redu

Come here, please.	**Дођите, молим вас.** Dođite, molim vas
I have some questions for you.	**Имам питања за вас.** Imam pitanja za vas
Wait a moment, please.	**Сачекајте, молим вас.** Sačekajte, molim vas
Do you have any I.D.?	**Имате ли исправе?** Imate li isprave?
Thanks. You can leave now.	**Хвала. Можете ићи.** Hvala. Možete ići
Hands behind your head!	**Руке иза главе!** Ruke iza glave!
You're under arrest!	**Ухапшени сте!** Uhapšeni ste!

Health problems

Please help me.	**Молим вас, помозите ми.** Molim vas, pomozite mi
I don't feel well.	**Не осећам се добро.** Ne osećam se dobro
My husband doesn't feel well.	**Мој муж се не осећа добро.** Moj muž se ne oseća dobro
My son ...	**Мој син ...** Moj sin ...
My father ...	**Мој отац ...** Moj otac ...
My wife doesn't feel well.	**Моја жена се не осећа добро.** Moja žena se ne oseća dobro
My daughter ...	**Моја ћерка ...** Moja ćerka ...
My mother ...	**Моја мајка ...** Moja majka ...
I've got a ...	**Боли ме ...** Boli me ...
headache	**глава** glava
sore throat	**грло** grlo
stomach ache	**стомак** stomak
toothache	**зуб** zub
I feel dizzy.	**Врти ми се у глави.** Vrti mi se u glavi
He has a fever.	**Он има температуру.** On ima temperaturu
She has a fever.	**Она има температуру.** Ona ima temperaturu
I can't breathe.	**Не могу да дишем.** Ne mogu da dišem
I'm short of breath.	**Не могу да удахнем.** Ne mogu da udahnem
I am asthmatic.	**Ја сам асматичар /асматичарка/.** Ja sam asmatičar /asmatičarka/
I am diabetic.	**Ја сам дијабетичар /дијабетичарка/.** Ja sam dijabetičar /dijabetičarka/

I can't sleep.	**Не могу да спавам.** Ne mogu da spavam
food poisoning	**тровање храном** trovanje hranom

It hurts here.	**Овде ме боли.** Ovde me boli
Help me!	**Помозите ми!** Pomozite mi!
I am here!	**Овде сам!** Ovde sam!
We are here!	**Овде смо!** Ovde smo!
Get me out of here!	**Вадите ме одавде!** Vadite me odavde!
I need a doctor.	**Потребан ми је лекар.** Potreban mi je lekar
I can't move.	**Не могу да се померим.** Ne mogu da se pomerim
I can't move my legs.	**Не могу да померам ноге.** Ne mogu da pomeram noge

I have a wound.	**Имам рану.** Imam ranu
Is it serious?	**Да ли је озбиљно?** Da li je ozbiljno?
My documents are in my pocket.	**Документа су ми у џепу.** Dokumenta su mi u džepu
Calm down!	**Смирите се!** Smirite se!
May I use your phone?	**Могу ли да се послужим вашим телефоном?** Mogu li da se poslužim vašim telefonom?

Call an ambulance!	**Позовите хитну помоћ!** Pozovite hitnu pomoć!
It's urgent!	**Хитно је!** Hitno je!
It's an emergency!	**Хитан случај!** Hitan slučaj!
Please hurry up!	**Молим вас, пожурите!** Molim vas, požurite!
Would you please call a doctor?	**Молим вас, зовите доктора?** Molim vas, zovite doktora?
Where is the hospital?	**Где је болница?** Gde je bolnica?

How are you feeling?	**Како се осећате?** Kako se osećate?
Are you all right?	**Да ли сте добро?** Da li ste dobro?

What's happened?	**Шта се десило?** Šta se desilo?
I feel better now.	**Сада се осећам боље.** Sada se osećam bolje
It's OK.	**OK је.** OK je
It's all right.	**У реду је.** U redu je

At the pharmacy

pharmacy (drugstore)	**апотека** apoteka
24-hour pharmacy	**дежурна апотека** dežurna apoteka
Where is the closest pharmacy?	**Где је најближа апотека?** Gde je najbliža apoteka?
Is it open now?	**Да ли је отворена сада?** Da li je otvorena sada?
At what time does it open?	**Када се отвара?** Kada se otvara?
At what time does it close?	**Када се затвара?** Kada se zatvara?
Is it far?	**Да ли је далеко?** Da li je daleko?
Can I get there on foot?	**Могу ли до тамо пешке?** Mogu li do tamo peške?
Can you show me on the map?	**Можете ли да ми покажете на мапи?** Možete li da mi pokažete na mapi?
Please give me something for …	**Молим вас, дајте ми нешто за …** Molim vas, dajte mi nešto za …
a headache	**главобољу** glavobolju
a cough	**кашаљ** kašalj
a cold	**прехладу** prehladu
the flu	**грип** grip
a fever	**температуру** temperaturu
a stomach ache	**стомачне тегобе** stomačne tegobe
nausea	**мучнину** mučninu
diarrhea	**дијареју** dijareju
constipation	**констипацију** konstipaciju
pain in the back	**болове у леђима** bolove u leđima

chest pain	**болове у грудима** bolove u grudima
side stitch	**бол у боку** bol u boku
abdominal pain	**бол у стомаку** bol u stomaku

pill	**пилула** pilula
ointment, cream	**маст, крема** mast, krema
syrup	**сируп** sirup
spray	**спреј** sprej
drops	**капи** kapi

You need to go to the hospital.	**Морате у болницу.** Morate u bolnicu
health insurance	**здравствено осигурање** zdravstveno osiguranje
prescription	**рецепт** recept
insect repellant	**нешто против инсеката** nešto protiv insekata
Band Aid	**фластер** flaster

The bare minimum

Excuse me, …	**Извините, …** Izvinite, …
Hello.	**Добар дан.** Dobar dan
Thank you.	**Хвала вам.** Hvala vam
Good bye.	**Довиђења.** Doviđenja
Yes.	**Да.** Da
No.	**Не.** Ne
I don't know.	**Не знам.** Ne znam
Where? | Where to? | When?	**Где? | Куда? | Када?** Gde? | Kuda? | Kada?
I need …	**Треба ми …** Treba mi …
I want …	**Хоћу …** Hoću …
Do you have …?	**Имате ли …?** Imate li …?
Is there a … here?	**Да ли овде постоји …?** Da li ovde postoji …?
May I …?	**Смем ли …?** Smem li …?
…, please (polite request)	**молим** molim
I'm looking for …	**Тражим …** Tražim …
restroom	**тоалет** toalet
ATM	**банкомат** bankomat
pharmacy (drugstore)	**апотеку** apoteku
hospital	**болницу** bolnicu
police station	**полицијску станицу** policijsku stanicu
subway	**метро** metro

taxi	**такси** taksi
train station	**железничку станицу** železničku stanicu

My name is …	**Ja се зовем …** Ja se zovem …
What's your name?	**Како се ви зовете?** Kako se vi zovete?
Could you please help me?	**Да ли бисте, молим вас, могли да ми помогнете?** Da li biste, molim vas, mogli da mi pomognete?
I've got a problem.	**Имам проблем.** Imam problem
I don't feel well.	**Не осећам се добро.** Ne osećam se dobro
Call an ambulance!	**Позовите хитну помоћ!** Pozovite hitnu pomoć!
May I make a call?	**Смем ли да телефонирам?** Smem li da telefoniram?

I'm sorry.	**Извините …** Izvinite …
You're welcome.	**Нема на чему.** Nema na čemu

I, me	**ja, мене** ja, mene
you (inform.)	**ти** ti
he	**он** on
she	**она** ona
they (masc.)	**они** oni
they (fem.)	**оне** one
we	**ми** mi
you (pl)	**ви** vi
you (sg, form.)	**ви** vi

ENTRANCE	**УЛАЗ** ULAZ
EXIT	**ИЗЛАЗ** IZLAZ
OUT OF ORDER	**НЕ РАДИ** NE RADI

CLOSED

ЗАТВОРЕНО
ZATVORENO

OPEN

ОТВОРЕНО
OTVORENO

FOR WOMEN

ЗА ЖЕНЕ
ZA ŽENE

FOR MEN

ЗА МУШКАРЦЕ
ZA MUŠKARCE

CONCISE DICTIONARY

This section contains more than 1,500 useful words arranged alphabetically. The dictionary includes a lot of gastronomic terms and will be helpful when ordering food at a restaurant or buying groceries

T&P Books Publishing

DICTIONARY CONTENTS

T&P Books Publishing

T&P Books Publishing

time	време (с)	vreme
hour	сат (м)	sat
half an hour	пола (ж) сата	pola sata
minute	минут (м)	minut
second	секунд (м)	sekund

today (adv)	данас	danas
tomorrow (adv)	сутра	sutra
yesterday (adv)	јуче	juče

Monday	понедељак (м)	ponedeljak
Tuesday	уторак (м)	utorak
Wednesday	среда (ж)	sreda
Thursday	четвртак (м)	četvrtak
Friday	петак (м)	petak
Saturday	субота (ж)	subota
Sunday	недеља (ж)	nedelja

day	дан (м)	dan
working day	радни дан (м)	radni dan
public holiday	празничан дан (м)	prazničan dan
weekend	викенд (м)	vikend

week	недеља (ж)	nedelja
last week (adv)	прошле недеље	prošle nedelje
next week (adv)	следеће недеље	sledeće nedelje

| sunrise | излазак (м) сунца | izlazak sunca |
| sunset | залазак (м) сунца | zalazak sunca |

| in the morning | ујутру | ujutru |
| in the afternoon | поподне | popodne |

| in the evening | увече | uveče |
| tonight (this evening) | вечерас | večeras |

| at night | ноћу | noću |
| midnight | поноћ (ж) | ponoć |

January	јануар (м)	januar
February	фебруар (м)	februar
March	март (м)	mart
April	април (м)	april
May	мај (м)	maj
June	јун (м), јуни (м)	jun, juni

July	јули (м)	juli
August	август (м)	avgust
September	септембар (м)	septembar
October	октобар (м)	oktobar
November	новембар (м)	novembar
December	децембар (м)	decembar
in spring	у пролеће	u proleće
in summer	лети	leti
in fall	у јесен	u jesen
in winter	зими	zimi
month	месец (м)	mesec
season (summer, etc.)	сезона (ж)	sezona
year	година (ж)	godina
century	век (м)	vek

2. Numbers. Numerals

digit, figure	цифра (ж)	cifra
number	број (м)	broj
minus sign	минус (м)	minus
plus sign	плус (м)	plus
sum, total	збир (м)	zbir
first (adj)	први	prvi
second (adj)	други	drugi
third (adj)	трећи	treći
0 zero	нула	nula
1 one	један	jedan
2 two	два	dva
3 three	три	tri
4 four	четири	četiri
5 five	пет	pet
6 six	шест	šest
7 seven	седам	sedam
8 eight	осам	osam
9 nine	девет	devet
10 ten	десет	deset
11 eleven	једанаест	jedanaest
12 twelve	дванаест	dvanaest
13 thirteen	тринаест	trinaest
14 fourteen	четрнаест	četrnaest
15 fifteen	петнаест	petnaest
16 sixteen	шеснаест	šesnaest
17 seventeen	седамнаест	sedamnaest

| 18 eighteen | осамнаест | osamnaest |
| 19 nineteen | деветнаест | devetnaest |

20 twenty	двадесет	dvadeset
30 thirty	тридесет	trideset
40 forty	четрдесет	četrdeset
50 fifty	педесет	pedeset

60 sixty	шездесет	šezdeset
70 seventy	седамдесет	sedamdeset
80 eighty	осамдесет	osamdeset
90 ninety	деведесет	devedeset

100 one hundred	сто	sto
200 two hundred	двеста	dvesta
300 three hundred	триста	trista
400 four hundred	четиристо	četiristo
500 five hundred	петсто	petsto

600 six hundred	шестсто	šeststo
700 seven hundred	седамсто	sedamsto
800 eight hundred	осамсто	osamsto
900 nine hundred	деветсто	devetsto
1000 one thousand	хиљада	hiljada

| 10000 ten thousand | десет хиљада | deset hiljada |
| one hundred thousand | сто хиљада | sto hiljada |

| million | милион (м) | milion |
| billion | милијарда (ж) | milijarda |

3. Humans. Family

man (adult male)	мушкарац (м)	muškarac
young man	младић (м)	mladić
teenager	тинејџер (м)	tinejdžer
woman	жена (ж)	žena
girl (young woman)	девојка (ж)	devojka

age	узраст (м)	uzrast
adult (adj)	одрастао (м)	odrastao
middle-aged (adj)	средњих година	srednjih godina
elderly (adj)	постарији	postariji
old (adj)	стар	star

old man	старац (м)	starac
old woman	старица (ж)	starica
retirement	пензија (ж)	penzija
to retire (from job)	пензионисати се	penzionisati se
retiree	пензионер (м)	penzioner

mother	мајка (ж)	majka
father	отац (м)	otac
son	син (м)	sin
daughter	кћи (ж)	kći
brother	брат (м)	brat
elder brother	старији брат (м)	stariji brat
younger brother	млађи брат (м)	mlađi brat
sister	сестра (ж)	sestra
elder sister	старија сестра (ж)	starija sestra
younger sister	млађа сестра (ж)	mlađa sestra

parents	родитељи (мн)	roditelji
child	дете (с)	dete
children	деца (с мн)	deca
stepmother	маћеха (ж)	maćeha
stepfather	очух (м)	očuh

grandmother	бака (ж)	baka
grandfather	деда (м)	deda
grandson	унук (м)	unuk
granddaughter	унука (ж)	unuka
grandchildren	унуци (мн)	unuci
uncle	ујак, стриц (м)	ujak, stric
aunt	ујна, стрина (ж)	ujna, strina
nephew	синовац (м)	sinovac
niece	синовица (ж)	sinovica

wife	жена (ж)	žena
husband	муж (м)	muž
married (masc.)	ожењен	oženjen
married (fem.)	удата	udata
widow	удовица (ж)	udovica
widower	удовац (м)	udovac

| name (first name) | име (с) | ime |
| surname (last name) | презиме (с) | prezime |

relative	рођак (м)	rođak
friend (masc.)	пријатељ (м)	prijatelj
friendship	пријатељство (с)	prijateljstvo

partner	партнер (м)	partner
superior (n)	начелник (м)	načelnik
colleague	колега (м)	kolega
neighbors	комшије (мн)	komšije

4. Human body

| organism (body) | организам (м) | organizam |
| body | тело (с) | telo |

heart	срце (c)	srce
blood	крв (ж)	krv
brain	мозак (м)	mozak
nerve	живац (м)	živac

bone	кост (ж)	kost
skeleton	костур (м)	kostur
spine (backbone)	кичма (ж)	kičma
rib	ребро (c)	rebro
skull	лобања (ж)	lobanja

muscle	мишић (м)	mišić
lungs	плућа (c мн)	pluća
skin	кожа (ж)	koža

head	глава (ж)	glava
face	лице (c)	lice
nose	нос (м)	nos
forehead	чело (c)	čelo
cheek	образ (м)	obraz

mouth	уста (c мн)	usta
tongue	језик (м)	jezik
tooth	зуб (м)	zub
lips	усне (ж мн)	usne
chin	брада (ж)	brada

ear	ухо (c)	uho
neck	врат (м)	vrat
throat	грло (c)	grlo

eye	око (c)	oko
pupil	зеница (ж)	zenica
eyebrow	обрва (ж)	obrva
eyelash	трепавица (ж)	trepavica

hair	коса (ж)	kosa
hairstyle	фризура (ж)	frizura
mustache	бркови (м мн)	brkovi
beard	брада (ж)	brada
to have (a beard, etc.)	носити	nositi
bald (adj)	ћелав	ćelav

hand	шака (ж)	šaka
arm	рука (ж)	ruka
finger	прст (м)	prst
nail	нокат (м)	nokat
palm	длан (ж)	dlan

shoulder	раме (c)	rame
leg	нога (ж)	noga
foot	стопало (c)	stopalo

| knee | колено (с) | koleno |
| heel | пета (ж) | peta |

back	леђа (мн)	leđa
waist	струк (м)	struk
beauty mark	младеж (м)	mladež
birthmark	белег, младеж (м)	beleg, mladež
(café au lait spot)		

5. Medicine. Diseases. Drugs

health	здравље (с)	zdravlje
well (not sick)	здрав	zdrav
sickness	болест (ж)	bolest
to be sick	боловати	bolovati
ill, sick (adj)	болестан	bolestan

cold (illness)	прехлада (ж)	prehlada
to catch a cold	прехладити се	prehladiti se
tonsillitis	ангина (ж)	angina
pneumonia	запаљење (с) плућа	zapaljenje pluća
flu, influenza	грип (м)	grip

runny nose (coryza)	кијавица (ж)	kijavica
cough	кашаљ (м)	kašalj
to cough (vi)	кашљати	kašljati
to sneeze (vi)	кијати	kijati

stroke	можданиudar (м)	moždani udar
heart attack	инфаркт (м)	infarkt
allergy	алергија (ж)	alergija
asthma	астма (ж)	astma
diabetes	дијабетес (м)	dijabetes

tumor	тумор (м)	tumor
cancer	рак (м)	rak
alcoholism	алкохолизам (м)	alkoholizam
AIDS	СИДА (ж)	SIDA
fever	грозница (ж)	groznica
seasickness	морска болест (ж)	morska bolest

bruise (hématome)	модрица (ж)	modrica
bump (lump)	чворуга (ж)	čvoruga
to limp (vi)	храмати	hramati
dislocation	ишчашење (с)	iščašenje
to dislocate (vt)	ишчашити	iščašiti

fracture	прелом (м)	prelom
burn (injury)	опекотина (ж)	opekotina
injury	повреда (ж)	povreda

| pain, ache | бол (м) | bol |
| toothache | зубобоља (ж) | zubobolja |

to sweat (perspire)	знојити се	znojiti se
deaf (adj)	глув	gluv
mute (adj)	нем	nem

immunity	имунитет (м)	imunitet
virus	вирус (м)	virus
microbe	микроб (м)	mikrob
bacterium	бактерија (ж)	bakterija
infection	инфекција (ж)	infekcija

hospital	болница (ж)	bolnica
cure	лечење (с)	lečenje
to vaccinate (vt)	вакцинисати се	vakcinisati se
to be in a coma	бити у коми	biti u komi
intensive care	интензивна нега (ж)	intenzivna nega
symptom	симптом (м)	simptom
pulse	пулс (м)	puls

6. Feelings. Emotions. Conversation

I, me	ја	ja
you	ти	ti
he	он	on
she	она	ona
it	оно	ono

we	ми	mi
you (to a group)	ви	vi
they (masc.)	они	oni
they (fem.)	оне	one

Hello! (fam.)	Здраво!	Zdravo!
Hello! (form.)	Добар дан!	Dobar dan!
Good morning!	Добро јутро!	Dobro jutro!
Good afternoon!	Добар дан!	Dobar dan!
Good evening!	Добро вече!	Dobro veče!

to say hello	поздрављати се	pozdravljati se
to greet (vt)	поздрављати	pozdravljati
How are you? (form.)	Како сте?	Kako ste?
How are you? (fam.)	Како си?	Kako si?
Goodbye! (form.)	Довиђења!	Doviđenja!
Bye! (fam.)	Здраво!	Zdravo!
Thank you!	Хвала!	Hvala!

| feelings | осећања (с мн) | osećanja |
| to be hungry | бити гладан | biti gladan |

| to be thirsty | бити жедан | biti žedan |
| tired (adj) | уморан | umoran |

to be worried	бити забринут	biti zabrinut
to be nervous	бити нервозан	biti nervozan
hope	нада (ж)	nada
to hope (vi, vt)	надати се	nadati se

character	карактер (м)	karakter
modest (adj)	скроман	skroman
lazy (adj)	лењ, ленив	lenj, leniv
generous (adj)	дарежљив	darežljiv
talented (adj)	талентован	talentovan

honest (adj)	часни	časni
serious (adj)	озбиљан	ozbiljan
shy, timid (adj)	стидљив	stidljiv
sincere (adj)	озбиљан	ozbiljan
coward	кукавица (м)	kukavica

to sleep (vi)	спавати	spavati
dream	сан (м)	san
bed	кревет (м)	krevet
pillow	јастук (м)	jastuk

insomnia	несаница (ж)	nesanica
to go to bed	ићи на спавање	ići na spavanje
nightmare	кошмар (м),	košmar,
	ноћна мора (ж)	noćna mora
alarm clock	будилник (м)	budilnik

smile	осмех (м)	osmeh
to smile (vi)	осмехивати се	osmehivati se
to laugh (vi)	смејати се	smejati se

quarrel	расправа, свађа (ж)	rasprava, svađa
insult	увреда (ж)	uvreda
resentment	кивност (ж)	kivnost
angry (mad)	љут	ljut

7. Clothing. Personal accessories

clothes	одећа (ж)	odeća
coat (overcoat)	капут (м)	kaput
fur coat	бунда (ж)	bunda
jacket (e.g., leather ~)	јакна (ж)	jakna
raincoat (trenchcoat, etc.)	кишни мантил (м)	kišni mantil

| shirt (button shirt) | кошуља (ж) | košulja |
| pants | панталоне (ж мн) | pantalone |

suit jacket	сако (м)	sako
suit	одело (с)	odelo
dress (frock)	хаљина (ж)	haljina
skirt	сукња (ж)	suknja
T-shirt	мајица (ж)	majica
bathrobe	баде мантил (м)	bade mantil
pajamas	пиџама (ж)	pidžama
workwear	радно одело (с)	radno odelo
underwear	доње рубље (с)	donje rublje
socks	чарапе (ж мн)	čarape
bra	грудњак (м)	grudnjak
pantyhose	грилонке (ж мн)	grilonke
stockings (thigh highs)	хулахопке (ж мн)	hulahopke
bathing suit	купаћи костим (м)	kupaći kostim
hat	капа (ж)	kapa
footwear	обућа (ж)	obuća
boots (e.g., cowboy ~)	чизме (ж мн)	čizme
heel	потпетица (ж)	potpetica
shoestring	пертла (ж)	pertla
shoe polish	крема (ж) за обућу	krema za obuću
cotton (n)	памук (м)	pamuk
wool (n)	вуна (ж)	vuna
fur (n)	крзно (с)	krzno
gloves	рукавице (ж мн)	rukavice
mittens	рукавице (ж мн)	rukavice
scarf (muffler)	шал (м)	šal
glasses (eyeglasses)	наочари (м мн)	naočari
umbrella	кишобран (м)	kišobran
tie (necktie)	кравата (ж)	kravata
handkerchief	џепна марамица (ж)	džepna maramica
comb	чешаљ (м)	češalj
hairbrush	четка (ж) за косу	četka za kosu
buckle	копча (ж)	kopča
belt	пас (м)	pas
purse	ташна (ж)	tašna
collar	оковратник (м)	okovratnik
pocket	џеп (м)	džep
sleeve	рукав (м)	rukav
fly (on trousers)	шлиц (м)	šlic
zipper (fastener)	рајсфешлус (м)	rajsfešlus
button	дугме (с)	dugme
to get dirty (vi)	искаљати се	iskaljati se
stain (mark, spot)	мрља (ж)	mrlja

8. City. Urban institutions

English	Serbian (Cyrillic)	Serbian (Latin)
store	продавница (ж)	prodavnica
shopping mall	тржни центар (м)	tržni centar
supermarket	супермаркет (м)	supermarket
shoe store	продавница (ж) обуће	prodavnica obuće
bookstore	књижара (ж)	knjižara
drugstore, pharmacy	апотека (ж)	apoteka
bakery	пекара (ж)	pekara
pastry shop	посластичарница (ж)	poslastičarnica
grocery store	бакалница (ж)	bakalnica
butcher shop	касапница (ж)	kasapnica
produce store	пиљарница (ж)	piljarnica
market	пијаца (ж)	pijaca
hair salon	фризерски салон (м)	frizerski salon
post office	пошта (ж)	pošta
dry cleaners	хемијско чишћење (с)	hemijsko čišćenje
circus	циркус (м)	cirkus
zoo	зоолошки врт (м)	zoološki vrt
theater	позориште (с)	pozorište
movie theater	биоскоп (м)	bioskop
museum	музеј (м)	muzej
library	библиотека (ж)	biblioteka
mosque	џамија (ж)	džamija
synagogue	синагога (ж)	sinagoga
cathedral	катедрала (ж)	katedrala
temple	храм (м)	hram
church	црква (ж)	crkva
college	институт (м)	institut
university	универзитет (м)	univerzitet
school	школа (ж)	škola
hotel	хотел (м)	hotel
bank	банка (ж)	banka
embassy	амбасада (ж)	ambasada
travel agency	туристичка агенција (ж)	turistička agencija
subway	метро (с)	metro
hospital	болница (ж)	bolnica
gas station	бензинска станица (ж)	benzinska stanica
parking lot	паркинг (м)	parking
ENTRANCE	УЛАЗ	ULAZ
EXIT	ИЗЛАЗ	IZLAZ
PUSH	ГУРНИ	GURNI
PULL	ВУЦИ	VUCI

| OPEN | **ОТВОРЕНО** | OTVORENO |
| CLOSED | **ЗАТВОРЕНО** | ZATVORENO |

monument	**споменик** (м)	spomenik
fortress	**тврђава** (ж)	tvrđava
palace	**палата** (ж), **дворац** (м)	palata, dvorac

medieval (adj)	**средњовекован**	srednjovekovan
ancient (adj)	**старински**	starinski
national (adj)	**народан**	narodan
famous (monument, etc.)	**чувен**	čuven

9. Money. Finances

money	**новац** (м)	novac
coin	**новчић** (м), **кованица** (ж)	novčić, kovanica
dollar	**долар** (м)	dolar
euro	**евро** (м)	evro

ATM	**банкомат** (м)	bankomat
currency exchange	**мењачица** (ж)	menjačica
exchange rate	**курс** (м)	kurs
cash	**готов новац** (м)	gotov novac

How much?	**Колико?**	Koliko?
to pay (vi, vt)	**платити**	platiti
payment	**плаћање** (с)	plaćanje
change (give the ~)	**кусур** (м)	kusur

price	**цена** (ж)	cena
discount	**попуст** (м)	popust
cheap (adj)	**јефтин**	jeftin
expensive (adj)	**скуп**	skup

bank	**банка** (ж)	banka
account	**рачун** (м)	račun
credit card	**кредитна карта** (ж)	kreditna karta
check	**чек** (м)	ček
to write a check	**написати чек**	napisati ček
checkbook	**чековна књижица** (ж)	čekovna knjižica

debt	**дуг** (м)	dug
debtor	**дужник** (м)	dužnik
to lend (money)	**дати у зајам**	dati u zajam
to borrow (vi, vt)	**узети у зајам**	uzeti u zajam

to rent (~ a tuxedo)	**изнајмити**	iznajmiti
on credit (adv)	**на кредит**	na kredit
wallet	**новчаник** (м)	novčanik
safe	**сеф** (м)	sef

| inheritance | наследство (с) | nasledstvo |
| fortune (wealth) | имовина (ж) | imovina |

tax	порез (м)	porez
fine	новчана казна (ж)	novčana kazna
to fine (vt)	казнити	kazniti

wholesale (adj)	велепродајни	veleprodajni
retail (adj)	малопродајни	maloprodajni
to insure (vt)	осигурати	osigurati
insurance	осигурање (с)	osiguranje

capital	капитал (м)	kapital
turnover	обрт (м)	obrt
stock (share)	акција (ж)	akcija
profit	добитак (м)	dobitak
profitable (adj)	профитабилан	profitabilan

crisis	криза (ж)	kriza
bankruptcy	банкротство (с)	bankrotstvo
to go bankrupt	банкротирати	bankrotirati

accountant	књиговођа (м)	knjigovođa
salary	плата (ж)	plata
bonus (money)	премија (ж)	premija

10. Transportation

bus	аутобус (м)	autobus
streetcar	трамвај (м)	tramvaj
trolley bus	тролејбус (м)	trolejbus

to go by ...	ићи ..., возити се ...	ići ..., voziti se ...
to get on (~ the bus)	ући у ...	ući u ...
to get off ...	сићи, изаћи из ...	sići, izaći iz ...

stop (e.g., bus ~)	станица (ж)	stanica
terminus	последња станица (ж)	poslednja stanica
schedule	ред (м) вожње	red vožnje
ticket	карта (ж)	karta
to be late (for ...)	каснити	kasniti

taxi, cab	такси (м)	taksi
by taxi	таксијем	taksijem
taxi stand	такси-станица (ж)	taksi-stanica

traffic	саобраћај (м)	saobraćaj
rush hour	шпиц (м)	špic
to park (vi)	паркирати се	parkirati se
subway	метро (м)	metro

station	станица (ж)	stanica
train	воз (м)	voz
train station	железничка станица (ж)	železnička stanica
rails	шине (ж мн)	šine
compartment	кабина (ж)	kabina
berth	лежај (м)	ležaj

airplane	авион (м)	avion
air ticket	авионска карта (ж)	avionska karta
airline	авио-компанија (ж)	avio-kompanija
airport	аеродром (м)	aerodrom

flight (act of flying)	лет (м)	let
luggage	пртљаг (м)	prtljag
luggage cart	колица (ж) за пртљаг	kolica za prtljag

ship	брод (м)	brod
cruise ship	брод (м) за крстарење	brod za krstarenje
yacht	јахта (ж)	jahta
boat (flat-bottomed ~)	чамац (м)	čamac

captain	капетан (м)	kapetan
cabin	кабина (ж)	kabina
port (harbor)	лука (ж)	luka

bicycle	бицикл (м)	bicikl
scooter	скутер (м)	skuter
motorcycle, bike	мотоцикл (м)	motocikl
pedal	педала (ж)	pedala
pump	пумпа (ж)	pumpa
wheel	точак (м)	točak

automobile, car	аутомобил (м)	automobil
ambulance	болничка кола (ж)	bolnička kola
truck	камион (м)	kamion
used (adj)	полован	polovan
car crash	саобраћајка (ж)	saobraćajka
repair	поправка (ж)	popravka

11. Food. Part 1

meat	месо (с)	meso
chicken	пилетина (ж)	piletina
duck	патка (ж)	patka
pork	свињетина (ж)	svinjetina
veal	телетина (ж)	teletina
lamb	јагњетина (ж)	jagnjetina
beef	говедина (ж)	govedina
sausage (bologna, pepperoni, etc.)	кобасица (ж)	kobasica

egg	jaje (c)	jaje
fish	риба (ж)	riba
cheese	сир (м)	sir
sugar	шећер (м)	šećer
salt	со (ж)	so

rice	пиринач (м)	pirinač
pasta (macaroni)	макароне (ж мн)	makarone
butter	маслац (м)	maslac
vegetable oil	зејтин (м)	zejtin
bread	хлеб (м)	hleb
chocolate (n)	чоколада (ж)	čokolada

wine	вино (c)	vino
coffee	кафа (ж)	kafa
milk	млеко (c)	mleko
juice	сок (м)	sok

| beer | пиво (c) | pivo |
| tea | чај (м) | čaj |

tomato	парадајз (м)	paradajz
cucumber	краставац (м)	krastavac
carrot	шаргарепа (ж)	šargarepa
potato	кромпир (м)	krompir

| onion | црни лук (м) | crni luk |
| garlic | бели лук, чешњак (м) | beli luk, češnjak |

cabbage	купус (м)	kupus
beetroot	цвекла (ж)	cvekla
eggplant	плави патлиџан (м)	plavi patlidžan
dill	мирођија (ж)	mirođija

| lettuce | зелена салата (ж) | zelena salata |
| corn (maize) | кукуруз (м) | kukuruz |

fruit	воћка (ж)	voćka
apple	јабука (ж)	jabuka
pear	крушка (ж)	kruška
lemon	лимун (м)	limun

| orange | наранџа (ж) | narandža |
| strawberry (garden ~) | јагода (ж) | jagoda |

plum	шљива (ж)	šljiva
raspberry	малина (ж)	malina
pineapple	ананас (м)	ananas
banana	банана (ж)	banana
watermelon	лубеница (ж)	lubenica
grape	грожђе (c)	grožđe
melon	диња (ж)	dinja

12. Food. Part 2

cuisine	кухиња (ж)	kuhinja
recipe	рецепт (м)	recept
food	храна (ж)	hrana

to have breakfast	доручковати	doručkovati
to have lunch	ручати	ručati
to have dinner	вечерати	večerati

taste, flavor	укус (м)	ukus
tasty (adj)	укусан	ukusan
cold (adj)	хладан	hladan
hot (adj)	врућ	vruć
sweet (sugary)	сладак	sladak
salty (adj)	слан	slan

sandwich (bread)	сендвич (м)	sendvič
side dish	прилог (м)	prilog
filling (for cake, pie)	фил (м)	fil
sauce	сос (м)	sos
piece (of cake, pie)	комад (м)	komad

diet	дијета (ж)	dijeta
vitamin	витамин (м)	vitamin
calorie	калорија (ж)	kalorija
vegetarian (n)	вегетаријанац (м)	vegetarijanac

restaurant	ресторан (м)	restoran
coffee house	кафић (м)	kafić
appetite	апетит (м)	apetit
Enjoy your meal!	Пријатно!	Prijatno!

waiter	конобар (м)	konobar
waitress	конобарица (ж)	konobarica
bartender	бармен (м)	barmen
menu	јеловник (м)	jelovnik

spoon	кашика (ж)	kašika
knife	нож (м)	nož
fork	виљушка (ж)	viljuška
cup (e.g., coffee ~)	шоља (ж)	šolja

plate (dinner ~)	тањир (м)	tanjir
saucer	тацна (ж)	tacna
napkin (on table)	салвета (ж)	salveta
toothpick	чачкалица (ж)	čačkalica

to order (meal)	наручити	naručiti
course, dish	јело (с)	jelo
portion	порција (ж)	porcija

appetizer	предјело (c)	predjelo
salad	салата (ж)	salata
soup	супа (ж)	supa

dessert	десерт (м)	desert
jam (whole fruit jam)	слатко (c)	slatko
ice-cream	сладолед (м)	sladoled

check	рачун (м)	račun
to pay the check	исплатити рачун	isplatiti račun
tip	бакшиш (м)	bakšiš

13. House. Apartment. Part 1

house	кућа (ж)	kuća
country house	сеоска кућа (ж)	seoska kuća
villa (seaside ~)	вила (ж)	vila

floor, story	спрат (м)	sprat
entrance	улаз (м)	ulaz
wall	зид (м)	zid
roof	кров (м)	krov
chimney	димњак (м)	dimnjak
attic (storage place)	таван (м)	tavan
window	прозор (м)	prozor
window ledge	прозорска даска (ж)	prozorska daska
balcony	балкон (м)	balkon

stairs (stairway)	степениште (c)	stepenište
mailbox	поштанско сандуче (c)	poštansko sanduče
garbage can	канта (ж) за ђубре	kanta za đubre
elevator	лифт (м)	lift

electricity	струја (ж)	struja
light bulb	сијалица (ж)	sijalica
switch	прекидач (м)	prekidač
wall socket	зидна утичница (ж)	zidna utičnica
fuse	осигурач (м)	osigurač

door	врата (ж мн)	vrata
handle, doorknob	квака (ж)	kvaka
key	кључ (м)	ključ
doormat	отирач (м)	otirač

door lock	брава (ж)	brava
doorbell	звонце (c)	zvonce
knock (at the door)	куцање (c)	kucanje
to knock (vi)	куцати	kucati
peephole	шпијунка (ж)	špijunka
yard	двориште (c)	dvorište

garden	врт (м)	vrt
swimming pool	базен (м)	bazen
gym (home gym)	теретана (ж)	teretana
tennis court	тениски терен (м)	teniski teren
garage	гаража (ж)	garaža

private property	приватан посед (м)	privatan posed
warning sign	знак (м) за упозорење	znak za upozorenje
security	обезбеђење (с)	obezbeđenje
security guard	чувар (м)	čuvar

renovations	реновирање (с)	renoviranje
to renovate (vt)	реновирати	renovirati
to put in order	довести у ред	dovesti u red
to paint (~ a wall)	фарбати	farbati
wallpaper	тапете (ж мн)	tapete
to varnish (vt)	лакирати	lakirati

pipe	цев (ж)	cev
tools	алати (м мн)	alati
basement	подрум (м)	podrum
sewerage (system)	канализација (ж)	kanalizacija

14. House. Apartment. Part 2

apartment	стан (м)	stan
room	соба (ж)	soba
bedroom	спаваћа соба (ж)	spavaća soba
dining room	трпезарија (ж)	trpezarija

living room	дневна соба (ж)	dnevna soba
study (home office)	кабинет (м)	kabinet
entry room	предсобље (с)	predsoblje
bathroom (room with a bath or shower)	купатило (с)	kupatilo
half bath	тоалет (м)	toalet

| floor | под (м) | pod |
| ceiling | плафон (м) | plafon |

to dust (vt)	брисати прашину	brisati prašinu
vacuum cleaner	усисивач (м)	usisivač
to vacuum (vt)	усисавати	usisavati

mop	џогер (м)	džoger
dust cloth	крпа (ж)	krpa
short broom	метла (ж)	metla
dustpan	ђубровник (м)	đubrovnik
furniture	намештај (м)	nameštaj
table	сто (м)	sto

| chair | столица (ж) | stolica |
| armchair | фотеља (ж) | fotelja |

bookcase	орман (м) за књиге	orman za knjige
shelf	полица (ж)	polica
wardrobe	орман (м)	orman

mirror	огледало (с)	ogledalo
carpet	тепих (м)	tepih
fireplace	камин (м)	kamin
drapes	завесе (ж мн)	zavese
table lamp	стона лампа (ж)	stona lampa
chandelier	лустер (м)	luster

kitchen	кухиња (ж)	kuhinja
gas stove (range)	плински шпорет (м)	plinski šporet
electric stove	електрички шпорет (м)	električki šporet
microwave oven	микроталасна рерна (ж)	mikrotalasna rerna

refrigerator	фрижидер (м)	frižider
freezer	замрзивач (м)	zamrzivač
dishwasher	машина (ж) за прање судова	mašina za pranje sudova

| faucet | славина (ж) | slavina |

| meat grinder | машина (ж) за млевење меса | mašina za mlevenje mesa |

juicer	соковник (м)	sokovnik
toaster	тостер (м)	toster
mixer	миксер (м)	mikser

coffee machine	апарат (м) за кафу	apparat za kafu
kettle	кувало, чајник (м)	kuvalo, čajnik
teapot	чајник (м)	čajnik

TV set	телевизор (м)	televizor
VCR (video recorder)	видео рекордер (м)	video rekorder
iron (e.g., steam ~)	пегла (ж)	pegla
telephone	телефон (м)	telefon

15. Professions. Social status

director	директор (м)	direktor
superior	претпостављен (м)	pretpostavljen
president	председник (м)	predsednik
assistant	помоћник (м)	pomoćnik
secretary	секретар (м), секретарица (ж)	sekretar, sekretarica
owner, proprietor	власник (м)	vlasnik
partner	партнер (м)	partner

stockholder	акционар (м)	akcionar
businessman	бизнисмен (м)	biznismen
millionaire	милионер (м)	milioner
billionaire	милијардер (м)	milijarder
actor	глумац (м)	glumac
architect	архитекта (м)	arhitekta
banker	банкар (м)	bankar
broker	брокер (м)	broker
veterinarian	ветеринар (м)	veterinar
doctor	лекар (м)	lekar
chambermaid	собарица (ж)	sobarica
designer	дизајнер (м)	dizajner
correspondent	кореспондент (м)	korespondent
delivery man	курир (м)	kurir
electrician	електричар (м)	električar
musician	музичар (м)	muzičar
babysitter	дадиља (ж)	dadilja
hairdresser	фризер (м)	frizer
herder, shepherd	чобанин, пастир (м)	čobanin, pastir
singer (masc.)	певач (м)	pevač
translator	преводилац (м)	prevodilac
writer	писац (м)	pisac
carpenter	столар (м)	stolar
cook	кувар (м)	kuvar
fireman	ватрогасац (м)	vatrogasac
police officer	полицајац (м)	policajac
mailman	поштар (м)	poštar
programmer	програмер (м)	programer
salesman (store staff)	продавац (м)	prodavac
worker	радник (м)	radnik
gardener	баштован (м)	baštovan
plumber	водоинсталатер (м)	vodoinstalater
dentist	стоматолог (м)	stomatolog
flight attendant (fem.)	стјуардеса (ж)	stjuardesa
dancer (masc.)	плесач (м)	plesač
bodyguard	телохранитељ (м)	telohranitelj
scientist	научник (м)	naučnik
schoolteacher	учитељ (м)	učitelj
farmer	фармер (м)	farmer
surgeon	хирург (м)	hirurg
miner	рудар (м)	rudar
chef (kitchen chef)	главни кувар (м)	glavni kuvar
driver	возач (м)	vozač

16. Sport

kind of sports	врста (ж) спорта	vrsta sporta
soccer	фудбал (м)	fudbal
hockey	хокеј (м)	hokej
basketball	кошарка (ж)	košarka
baseball	бејзбол (м)	bejzbol
volleyball	одбојка (ж)	odbojka
boxing	бокс (м)	boks
wrestling	рвање (с)	rvanje
tennis	тенис (м)	tenis
swimming	пливање (с)	plivanje
chess	шах (м)	šah
running	трчање (с)	trčanje
athletics	лака атлетика (ж)	laka atletika
figure skating	уметничко клизање (с)	umetničko klizanje
cycling	бициклизам (м)	biciklizam
billiards	билијар (м)	bilijar
bodybuilding	бодибилдинг (м)	bodibilding
golf	голф (м)	golf
scuba diving	роњење (с)	ronjenje
sailing	једрење (с)	jedrenje
archery	стреличарство (с)	streličarstvo
period, half	полувреме (с)	poluvreme
half-time	полувреме (с)	poluvreme
tie	нерешена игра (ж)	nerešena igra
to tie (vi)	играти нерешено	igrati nerešeno
treadmill	тркачка стаза (ж)	trkačka staza
player	играч (м)	igrač
substitute	резервни играч (м)	rezervni igrač
substitutes bench	резервна клупа (ж)	rezervna klupa
match	меч (м)	meč
goal	гол (м)	gol
goalkeeper	голман (м)	golman
goal (score)	гол (м)	gol
Olympic Games	Олимпијске игре (ж мн)	Olimpijske igre
to set a record	поставити рекорд	postaviti rekord
final	финале (с)	finale
champion	шампион (м)	šampion
championship	првенство (с)	prvenstvo
winner	победник (м)	pobednik
victory	победа (ж)	pobeda
to win (vi)	победити	pobediti

to lose (not win)	изгубити	izgubiti
medal	медаља (ж)	medalja
first place	прво место (с)	prvo mesto
second place	друго место (с)	drugo mesto
third place	треће место (с)	treće mesto
stadium	стадион (м)	stadion
fan, supporter	навијач (м)	navijač
trainer, coach	тренер (м)	trener
training	тренинг (м), тренирање (с)	trening, treniranje

17. Foreign languages. Orthography

language	језик (м)	jezik
to study (vt)	студирати	studirati
pronunciation	изговор (м)	izgovor
accent	нагласак (м)	naglasak
noun	именица (ж)	imenica
adjective	придев (м)	pridev
verb	глагол (м)	glagol
adverb	прилог (м)	prilog
pronoun	заменица (ж)	zamenica
interjection	ускличник (м)	uskličnik
preposition	предлог (м)	predlog
root	корен (м)	koren
ending	наставак (м)	nastavak
prefix	префикс (м)	prefiks
syllable	слог (м)	slog
suffix	суфикс (м)	sufiks
stress mark	акцент (м)	akcent
period, dot	тачка (ж)	tačka
comma	зарез (м)	zarez
colon	две тачке (ж мн)	dve tačke
ellipsis	три тачке (ж мн)	tri tačke
question	питање (с)	pitanje
question mark	упитник (м)	upitnik
exclamation point	узвичник (м)	uzvičnik
in quotation marks	под наводницима	pod navodnicima
in parenthesis	у загради	u zagradi
letter	слово (с)	slovo
capital letter	велико слово (с)	veliko slovo
sentence	реченица (ж)	rečenica

group of words	група (ж) речи	grupa reči
expression	израз (м)	izraz
subject	субјекат (м)	subjekat
predicate	предикат (м)	predikat
line	ред (м)	red
paragraph	пасус (м)	pasus
synonym	синоним (м)	sinonim
antonym	антоним (м)	antonim
exception	изузетак (м)	izuzetak
to underline (vt)	подвући	podvući
rules	правила (с мн)	pravila
grammar	граматика (ж)	gramatika
vocabulary	лексикон (м)	leksikon
phonetics	фонетика (ж)	fonetika
alphabet	азбука, абецеда (ж)	azbuka, abeceda
textbook	уџбеник (м)	udžbenik
dictionary	речник (м)	rečnik
phrasebook	приручник (м) за конверзацију	priručnik za konverzaciju
word	реч (ж)	reč
meaning	смисао (м)	smisao
memory	памћење (с)	pamćenje

18. The Earth. Geography

the Earth	Земља (ж)	Zemlja
the globe (the Earth)	земљина кугла (ж)	zemljina kugla
planet	планета (ж)	planeta
geography	географија (ж)	geografija
nature	природа (ж)	priroda
map	мапа (ж)	mapa
atlas	атлас (м)	atlas
in the north	на северу	na severu
in the south	на југу	na jugu
in the west	на западу	na zapadu
in the east	на истоку	na istoku
sea	море (с)	more
ocean	океан (м)	okean
gulf (bay)	залив (м)	zaliv
straits	мореуз (м)	moreuz
continent (mainland)	континент (м)	kontinent
island	острво (с)	ostrvo

| peninsula | полуострво (c) | poluostrvo |
| archipelago | архипелаг (м) | arhipelag |

harbor	лука (ж)	luka
coral reef	корални гребен (м)	koralni greben
shore	обала (ж)	obala
coast	приморје (c)	primorje

| flow (flood tide) | плима (ж) | plima |
| ebb (ebb tide) | осека (ж) | oseka |

latitude	ширина (ж)	širina
longitude	дужина (ж)	dužina
parallel	паралела (ж)	paralela
equator	екватор (м)	ekvator

sky	небо (c)	nebo
horizon	хоризонт (м)	horizont
atmosphere	атмосфера (ж)	atmosfera

mountain	планина (ж)	planina
summit, top	врх (м)	vrh
cliff	литица (ж)	litica
hill	брег (м)	breg

volcano	вулкан (м)	vulkan
glacier	леденик (м)	ledenik
waterfall	водопад (м)	vodopad
plain	равница (ж)	ravnica

river	река (ж)	reka
spring (natural source)	извор (м)	izvor
bank (of river)	обала (ж)	obala
downstream (adv)	низводно	nizvodno
upstream (adv)	узводно	uzvodno

lake	језеро (c)	jezero
dam	брана (ж)	brana
canal	канал (м)	kanal
swamp (marshland)	мочвара (ж)	močvara
ice	лед (м)	led

19. Countries of the world. Part 1

Europe	Европа (ж)	Evropa
European Union	Европска унија (ж)	Evropska unija
European (n)	европљанин (м)	evropljanin
European (adj)	европски	evropski
Austria	Аустрија (ж)	Austrija
Great Britain	Велика Британија (ж)	Velika Britanija

England	Енглеска (ж)	Engleska
Belgium	Белгија (ж)	Belgija
Germany	Немачка (ж)	Nemačka
Netherlands	Холандија (ж)	Holandija
Holland	Холандија (ж)	Holandija
Greece	Грчка (ж)	Grčka
Denmark	Данска (ж)	Danska
Ireland	Ирска (ж)	Irska
Iceland	Исланд (м)	Island
Spain	Шпанија (ж)	Španija
Italy	Италија (ж)	Italija
Cyprus	Кипар (м)	Kipar
Malta	Малта (ж)	Malta
Norway	Норвешка (ж)	Norveška
Portugal	Португалија (ж)	Portugalija
Finland	Финска (ж)	Finska
France	Француска (ж)	Francuska
Sweden	Шведска (ж)	Švedska
Switzerland	Швајцарска (ж)	Švajcarska
Scotland	Шкотска (ж)	Škotska
Vatican	Ватикан (м)	Vatikan
Liechtenstein	Лихтенштајн (м)	Lihtenštajn
Luxembourg	Луксембург (м)	Luksemburg
Monaco	Монако (м)	Monako
Albania	Албанија (ж)	Albanija
Bulgaria	Бугарска (ж)	Bugarska
Hungary	Мађарска (ж)	Mađarska
Latvia	Летонија (ж)	Letonija
Lithuania	Литванија (ж)	Litvanija
Poland	Пољска (ж)	Poljska
Romania	Румунија (ж)	Rumunija
Serbia	Србија (ж)	Srbija
Slovakia	Словачка (ж)	Slovačka
Croatia	Хрвастка (ж)	Hrvastka
Czech Republic	Чешка република (ж)	Češka republika
Estonia	Естонија (ж)	Estonija
Bosnia and Herzegovina	Босна и Херцеговина (ж)	Bosna i Hercegovina
Macedonia (Republic of ~)	Македонија (ж)	Makedonija
Slovenia	Словенија (ж)	Slovenija
Montenegro	Црна Гора (ж)	Crna Gora
Belarus	Белорусија (ж)	Belorusija
Moldova, Moldavia	Молдавија (ж)	Moldavija
Russia	Русија (ж)	Rusija
Ukraine	Украјина (ж)	Ukrajina

20. Countries of the world. Part 2

Asia	Азија (ж)	Azija
Vietnam	Вијетнам (м)	Vijetnam
India	Индија (ж)	Indija
Israel	Израел (м)	Izrael
China	Кина (ж)	Kina

Lebanon	Либан (м)	Liban
Mongolia	Монголија (ж)	Mongolija
Malaysia	Малејзија (ж)	Malejzija
Pakistan	Пакистан (м)	Pakistan
Saudi Arabia	Саудијска Арабија (ж)	Saudijska Arabija

Thailand	Тајланд (м)	Tajland
Taiwan	Тајван (м)	Tajvan
Turkey	Турска (ж)	Turska
Japan	Јапан (м)	Japan
Afghanistan	Авганистан (м)	Avganistan

Bangladesh	Бангладеш (м)	Bangladeš
Indonesia	Индонезија (ж)	Indonezija
Jordan	Јордан (м)	Jordan
Iraq	Ирак (м)	Irak
Iran	Иран (м)	Iran

Cambodia	Камбоџа (ж)	Kambodža
Kuwait	Кувајт (м)	Kuvajt
Laos	Лаос (м)	Laos
Myanmar	Мијанмар (м)	Mijanmar
Nepal	Непал (м)	Nepal

United Arab Emirates	Уједињени Арапски Емирати (м мн)	Ujedinjeni Arapski Emirati
Syria	Сирија (ж)	Sirija
Palestine	Палестина (ж)	Palestina
South Korea	Јужна Кореја (ж)	Južna Koreja
North Korea	Северна Кореја (ж)	Severna Koreja

United States of America	Сједињене Америчке Државе (ж мн)	Sjedinjene Američke Države
Canada	Канада (ж)	Kanada
Mexico	Мексико (м)	Meksiko
Argentina	Аргентина (ж)	Argentina
Brazil	Бразил (м)	Brazil

Colombia	Колумбија (ж)	Kolumbija
Cuba	Куба (ж)	Kuba
Chile	Чиле (м)	Čile
Venezuela	Венецуела (ж)	Venecuela
Ecuador	Еквадор (м)	Ekvador

The Bahamas	Бахами (с мн)	Bahami
Panama	Панама (ж)	Panama
Egypt	Египат (м)	Egipat
Morocco	Мароко (м)	Maroko
Tunisia	Тунис (м)	Tunis
Kenya	Кенија (ж)	Kenija
Libya	Либија (ж)	Libija
South Africa	Јужноафричка република (ж)	Južnoafrička republika
Australia	Аустралија (ж)	Australija
New Zealand	Нови Зеланд (м)	Novi Zeland

21. Weather. Natural disasters

weather	време (с)	vreme
weather forecast	временска прогноза (ж)	vremenska prognoza
temperature	температура (ж)	temperatura
thermometer	термометар (м)	termometar
barometer	барометар (м)	barometar
sun	сунце (с)	sunce
to shine (vi)	сијати	sijati
sunny (day)	сунчан	sunčan
to come up (vi)	изаћи	izaći
to set (vi)	заћи	zaći
rain	киша (ж)	kiša
it's raining	пада киша	pada kiša
pouring rain	јака киша (ж)	jaka kiša
rain cloud	кишни облак (м)	kišni oblak
puddle	бара (ж)	bara
to get wet (in rain)	покиснути	pokisnuti
thunderstorm	олуја (ж)	oluja
lightning (~ strike)	муња (ж)	munja
to flash (vi)	севати	sevati
thunder	гром (м)	grom
it's thundering	грми	grmi
hail	град (м)	grad
it's hailing	пада град	pada grad
heat (extreme ~)	вручина (ж)	vrućina
it's hot	вруће је	vruće je
it's warm	топло је	toplo je
it's cold	хладно је	hladno je
fog (mist)	магла (ж)	magla
foggy	магловит	maglovit
cloud	облак (м)	oblak

| cloudy (adj) | облачан | oblačan |
| humidity | влажност (ж) | vlažnost |

snow	снег (м)	sneg
it's snowing	пада снег	pada sneg
frost (severe ~, freezing cold)	мраз (м)	mraz
below zero (adv)	испод нуле	ispod nule
hoarfrost	иње (с)	inje

bad weather	невреме (с)	nevreme
disaster	катастрофа (ж)	katastrofa
flood, inundation	поплава (ж)	poplava
avalanche	лавина (ж)	lavina
earthquake	земљотрес (м)	zemljotres

tremor, quake	потрес (м)	potres
epicenter	епицентар (м)	epicentar
eruption	ерупција (ж)	erupcija
lava	лава (ж)	lava

tornado	торнадо (м)	tornado
twister	пијавица (ж)	pijavica
hurricane	ураган (м)	uragan
tsunami	цунами (м)	cunami
cyclone	циклон (м)	ciklon

22. Animals. Part 1

| animal | животиња (ж) | životinja |
| predator | грабљивац (м) | grabljivac |

tiger	тигар (м)	tigar
lion	лав (м)	lav
wolf	вук (м)	vuk
fox	лисица (ж)	lisica
jaguar	јагуар (м)	jaguar

lynx	рис (м)	ris
coyote	којот (м)	kojot
jackal	шакал (м)	šakal
hyena	хијена (ж)	hijena

squirrel	веверица (ж)	veverica
hedgehog	јеж (м)	jež
rabbit	кунић (м)	kunić
raccoon	ракун (м)	rakun

| hamster | хрчак (м) | hrčak |
| mole | кртица (ж) | krtica |

mouse	миш (м)	miš
rat	пацов (м)	pacov
bat	слепи миш (м)	slepi miš

beaver	дабар (м)	dabar
horse	коњ (м)	konj
deer	јелен (м)	jelen
camel	камила (ж)	kamila
zebra	зебра (ж)	zebra

whale	кит (м)	kit
seal	фока (ж)	foka
walrus	морж (м)	morž
dolphin	делфин (м)	delfin

bear	медвед (м)	medved
monkey	мајмун (м)	majmun
elephant	слон (м)	slon
rhinoceros	носорог (м)	nosorog
giraffe	жирафа (ж)	žirafa

hippopotamus	нилски коњ (м)	nilski konj
kangaroo	кенгур (м)	kengur
cat	мачка (ж)	mačka
dog	пас (м)	pas

cow	крава (ж)	krava
bull	бик (м)	bik
sheep (ewe)	овца (ж)	ovca
goat	коза (ж)	koza

donkey	магарац (м)	magarac
pig, hog	свиња (ж)	svinja
hen (chicken)	кокош (ж)	kokoš
rooster	певац (м)	pevac

duck	патка (ж)	patka
goose	гуска (ж)	guska
turkey (hen)	ћурка (ж)	ćurka
sheepdog	овчар (м)	ovčar

23. Animals. Part 2

bird	птица (ж)	ptica
pigeon	голуб (м)	golub
sparrow	врабац (м)	vrabac
tit (great tit)	сеница (ж)	senica
magpie	сврака (ж)	svraka
eagle	орао (м)	orao
hawk	јастреб (м)	jastreb

falcon	соко (м)	soko
swan	лабуд (м)	labud
crane	ждрал (м)	ždral
stork	рода (ж)	roda
parrot	папагај (м)	papagaj
peacock	паун (м)	paun
ostrich	ној (м)	noj

heron	чапља (ж)	čaplja
nightingale	славуј (м)	slavuj
swallow	ластавица (ж)	lastavica
woodpecker	детлић (м)	detlić
cuckoo	кукавица (ж)	kukavica
owl	сова (ж)	sova

penguin	пингвин (м)	pingvin
tuna	туњ (м)	tunj
trout	пастрмка (ж)	pastrmka
eel	јегуља (ж)	jegulja

shark	ајкула (ж)	ajkula
crab	морски рак (м)	morski rak
jellyfish	медуза (ж)	meduza
octopus	хоботница (ж)	hobotnica

starfish	морска звезда (ж)	morska zvezda
sea urchin	морски јеж (м)	morski jež
seahorse	морски коњић (м)	morski konjić
shrimp	морски рачић (м)	morski račić

snake	змија (ж)	zmija
viper	поскок (м)	poskok
lizard	гуштер (м)	gušter
iguana	игуана (ж)	iguana

| chameleon | камелеон (м) | kameleon |
| scorpion | шкорпија (ж) | škorpija |

turtle	корњача (ж)	kornjača
frog	жаба (ж)	žaba
crocodile	крокодил (м)	krokodil

| insect, bug | инсект (м) | insekt |
| butterfly | лептир (м) | leptir |

| ant | мрав (м) | mrav |
| fly | мува (ж) | muva |

mosquito	комарац (м)	komarac
beetle	буба (ж)	buba
bee	пчела (ж)	pčela
spider	паук (м)	pauk

24. Trees. Plants

tree	дрво (c)	drvo
birch	бреза (ж)	breza
oak	храст (м)	hrast
linden tree	липа (ж)	lipa
aspen	јасика (ж)	jasika
maple	јавор (м)	javor
spruce	јела (ж)	jela
pine	бор (м)	bor
cedar	кедар (м)	kedar
poplar	топола (ж)	topola
rowan	оскоруша (ж)	oskoruša
beech	буква (ж)	bukva
elm	брест (м)	brest
ash (tree)	јасен (м)	jasen
chestnut	кестен (м)	kesten
palm tree	палма (ж)	palma
bush	грм (м)	grm
mushroom	гљива, печурка (ж)	gljiva, pečurka
poisonous mushroom	отровна печурка (ж)	otrovna pečurka
cep (Boletus edulis)	вргањ (м)	vrganj
russula	глувара (ж)	gluvara
fly agaric	мухомор (м)	muhomor
death cap	отровна гљива (ж)	otrovna gljiva
flower	цвет (м)	cvet
bouquet (of flowers)	букет (ж)	buket
rose (flower)	ружа (ж)	ruža
tulip	лала (ж), тулипан (м)	lala, tulipan
carnation	каранфил (м)	karanfil
camomile	камилица (ж)	kamilica
cactus	кактус (м)	kaktus
lily of the valley	ђурђевак (м)	đurđevak
snowdrop	висибаба (ж)	visibaba
water lily	локвањ (м)	lokvanj
greenhouse (tropical ~)	стаклена башта (ж)	staklena bašta
lawn	травњак (м)	travnjak
flowerbed	цветна леја (ж)	cvetna leja
plant	биљка (ж)	biljka
grass	трава (ж)	trava
leaf	лист (м)	list
petal	латица (ж)	latica
stem	стабло (c)	stablo

young plant (shoot)	изданак (м)	izdanak
cereal crops	житарице (ж мн)	žitarice
wheat	пшеница (ж)	pšenica
rye	раж (ж)	raž
oats	овас (м)	ovas

millet	просо (с)	proso
barley	јечам (м)	ječam
corn	кукуруз (м)	kukuruz
rice	пиринач (м)	pirinač

25. Various useful words

balance (of situation)	равнотежа (ж)	ravnoteža
base (basis)	база (ж)	baza
beginning	почетак (м)	početak
category	категорија (ж)	kategorija

choice	избор (м)	izbor
coincidence	подударање (с)	podudaranje
comparison	поређење (с)	poređenje
degree (extent, amount)	степен (м)	stepen

development	развој (м)	razvoj
difference	разлика (ж)	razlika
effect (e.g., of drugs)	ефекат (м)	efekat
effort (exertion)	напор (м)	napor

element	елемент (м)	elemenat
example (illustration)	пример (м)	primer
fact	чињеница (ж)	činjenica
help	помоћ (ж)	pomoć

ideal	идеал (м)	ideal
kind (sort, type)	врста (ж)	vrsta
mistake, error	грешка (ж)	greška
moment	моменат (м)	momenat

obstacle	препрека (ж)	prepreka
part (~ of sth)	део (м)	deo
pause (break)	пауза (ж)	pauza
position	позиција (ж)	pozicija

problem	проблем (м)	problem
process	процес (м)	proces
progress	прогрес (м)	progres
property (quality)	својство	svojstvo
reaction	реакција (ж)	reakcija
risk	ризик (м)	rizik

secret	тајна (ж)	tajna
series	серија (ж)	serija
shape (outer form)	облик (м)	oblik
situation	ситуација (ж)	situacija
solution	решење (с)	rešenje
standard (adj)	стандардан	standardan
stop (pause)	застој, одмор (м)	zastoj, odmor
style	стил (м)	stil
system	систем (м)	sistem
table (chart)	таблица (ж)	tablica
tempo, rate	темпо (м)	tempo
term (word, expression)	термин (м)	termin
truth (e.g., moment of ~)	истина (ж)	istina
turn (please wait your ~)	ред (м)	red
urgent (adj)	хитан	hitan
utility (usefulness)	корист (ж)	korist
variant (alternative)	варијанта (ж)	varijanta
way (means, method)	начин (м)	način
zone	зона (ж)	zona

26. Modifiers. Adjectives. Part 1

additional (adj)	додатан	dodatan
ancient (~ civilization)	древни	drevni
artificial (adj)	вештачки	veštački
bad (adj)	лош, рђав	loš, rđav
beautiful (person)	леп	lep
big (in size)	велики	veliki
bitter (taste)	горак	gorak
blind (sightless)	слеп	slep
central (adj)	централни	centralni
children's (adj)	дечји	dečji
clandestine (secret)	илегалан	ilegalan
clean (free from dirt)	чист	čist
clever (smart)	паметан	pametan
compatible (adj)	компатибилан	kompatibilan
contented (satisfied)	задовољан	zadovoljan
dangerous (adj)	опасан	opasan
dead (not alive)	мртав	mrtav
dense (fog, smoke)	густ	gust
difficult (decision)	тежак	težak
dirty (not clean)	прљав	prljav
easy (not difficult)	лак	lak

empty (glass, room)	празан	prazan
exact (amount)	тачан	tačan
excellent (adj)	одличан	odličan

excessive (adj)	прекомеран	prekomeran
exterior (adj)	спољашњи	spoljašnji
fast (quick)	брз	brz
fertile (land, soil)	плодан	plodan
fragile (china, glass)	ломљив	lomljiv

free (at no cost)	бесплатан	besplatan
fresh (~ water)	слатка	slatka
frozen (food)	замрзнут	zamrznut
full (completely filled)	пун	pun
happy (adj)	срећан	srećan

hard (not soft)	тврд	tvrd
huge (adj)	огроман	ogroman
ill (sick, unwell)	болестан	bolestan
immobile (adj)	непокретан	nepokretan
important (adj)	важан	važan

interior (adj)	унутрашњи	unutrašnji
last (e.g., ~ week)	прошли	prošli
last (final)	последњи	poslednji
left (e.g., ~ side)	леви	levi
legal (legitimate)	законит	zakonit

light (in weight)	лак	lak
liquid (fluid)	течан	tečan
long (e.g., ~ hair)	дугачак	dugačak
loud (voice, etc.)	гласан	glasan
low (voice)	тих	tih

27. Modifiers. Adjectives. Part 2

main (principal)	главни	glavni
matt, matte	мат	mat
mysterious (adj)	загонетан	zagonetan
narrow (street, etc.)	узак	uzak
native (~ country)	родан, матичан	rodan, matičan

negative (~ response)	негативан	negativan
new (adj)	нов	nov
next (e.g., ~ week)	следећи	sledeći
normal (adj)	нормалан	normalan
not difficult (adj)	није сложен	nije složen

| obligatory (adj) | обавезан | obavezan |
| old (house) | стар | star |

open (adj)	отворен	otvoren
opposite (adj)	супротан	suprotan
ordinary (usual)	обичан	običan
original (unusual)	оригиналан	originalan
personal (adj)	личан	ličan
polite (adj)	учтив	učtiv
poor (not rich)	сиромашан	siromašan
possible (adj)	могућ	moguć
principal (main)	основни	osnovni
probable (adj)	вероватан	verovatan
prolonged (e.g., ~ applause)	дуготрајан	dugotrajan
public (open to all)	јаван	javan
rare (adj)	редак	redak
raw (uncooked)	сиров	sirov
right (not left)	десни	desni
ripe (fruit)	зрео	zreo
risky (adj)	ризичан	rizičan
sad (~ look)	тужан	tužan
second hand (adj)	полован	polovan
shallow (water)	плитак	plitak
sharp (blade, etc.)	оштар	oštar
short (in length)	кратак	kratak
similar (adj)	сличан	sličan
small (in size)	мали	mali
smooth (surface)	гладак	gladak
soft (~ toys)	мек, мекан	mek, mekan
solid (~ wall)	чврст	čvrst
sour (flavor, taste)	кисео	kiseo
spacious (house, etc.)	просторан	prostoran
special (adj)	специјалан	specijalan
straight (line, road)	прав	prav
strong (person)	снажан	snažan
stupid (foolish)	глуп	glup
superb, perfect (adj)	превасходан	prevashodan
sweet (sugary)	сладак	sladak
tan (adj)	преплануо	preplanuo
tasty (delicious)	укусан	ukusan
unclear (adj)	нејасан	nejasan

28. Verbs. Part 1

to accuse (vt)	оптужити, окривљавати	optužiti, okrivljavati
to agree (say yes)	слагати се	slagati se

to announce (vt)	објавити	objaviti
to answer (vi, vt)	одговарати	odgovarati
to apologize (vi)	извињавати се	izvinjavati se
to arrive (vi)	долазити	dolaziti
to ask (~ oneself)	питати	pitati
to be absent	одсуствовати	odsustvovati
to be afraid	плашити се, бојати се	plašiti se, bojati se
to be born	родити се	roditi se
to be in a hurry	журити	žuriti
to beat (to hit)	тући	tući
to begin (vt)	почињати	počinjati
to believe (in God)	веровати	verovati
to belong to …	припадати	pripadati
to break (split into pieces)	ломити	lomiti
to build (vt)	градити	graditi
to buy (purchase)	куповати	kupovati
can (v aux)	моћи	moći
can (v aux)	моћи	moći
to cancel (call off)	отказати	otkazati
to catch (vt)	хватати	hvatati
to change (vt)	променити	promeniti
to check (to examine)	проверити	proveriti
to choose (select)	бирати	birati
to clean up (tidy)	поспремити	pospremiti
to close (vt)	затворити	zatvoriti
to compare (vt)	упоређивати	upoređivati
to complain (vi, vt)	жалити се	žaliti se
to confirm (vt)	потврдити	potvrditi
to congratulate (vt)	честитати	čestitati
to cook (dinner)	кувати	kuvati
to copy (vt)	копирати	kopirati
to cost (vt)	коштати	koštati
to count (add up)	сабирати	sabirati
to count on …	рачунати на …	računati na …
to create (vt)	направити	napraviti
to cry (weep)	плакати	plakati
to dance (vi, vt)	плесати	plesati
to deceive (vi, vt)	обманути	obmanuti
to decide (~ to do sth)	одлучити се	odlučiti se
to delete (vt)	избрисати	izbrisati
to demand (request firmly)	захтевати, тражити	zahtevati, tražiti
to deny (vt)	порећи	poreći
to depend on …	зависити од …	zavisiti od …
to despise (vt)	презирати	prezirati

to die (vi)	умрети	umreti
to dig (vt)	копати	kopati
to disappear (vi)	ишчезнути	iščeznuti
to discuss (vt)	расправљати	raspravljati
to disturb (vt)	сметати	smetati

29. Verbs. Part 2

to dive (vi)	ронити	roniti
to divorce (vi)	развести се	razvesti se
to do (vt)	радити	raditi
to doubt (have doubts)	сумњати	sumnjati
to drink (vi, vt)	пити	piti

to drop (let fall)	испустити	ispustiti
to dry (clothes, hair)	сушити	sušiti
to eat (vi, vt)	јести	jesti
to end (~ a relationship)	окончати	okončati
to excuse (forgive)	извинити	izviniti

to exist (vi)	постојати	postojati
to expect (foresee)	предвидети	predvideti
to explain (vt)	објашњавати	objašnjavati
to fall (vi)	падати	padati
to fight (street fight, etc.)	тући се	tući se
to find (vt)	наћи	naći

to finish (vt)	завршавати	završavati
to fly (vi)	летети	leteti
to forbid (vt)	забранити	zabraniti
to forget (vi, vt)	заборављати	zaboravljati
to forgive (vt)	опраштати	opraštati

to get tired	уморити се	umoriti se
to give (vt)	давати	davati
to go (on foot)	ићи	ići
to hate (vt)	мрзети	mrzeti

to have (vt)	имати	imati
to have breakfast	доручковати	doručkovati
to have dinner	вечерати	večerati
to have lunch	ручати	ručati

to hear (vt)	чути	čuti
to help (vt)	помагати	pomagati
to hide (vt)	крити	kriti
to hope (vi, vt)	надати се	nadati se
to hunt (vi, vt)	ловити	loviti
to hurry (vi)	журити се	žuriti se
to insist (vi, vt)	инсистирати	insistirati

to insult (vt)	вређати	vređati
to invite (vt)	позвати	pozvati
to joke (vi)	шалити се	šaliti se
to keep (vt)	чувати	čuvati

to kill (vt)	убити	ubiti
to know (sb)	знати	znati
to know (sth)	знати	znati
to like (I like …)	свиђати се	sviđati se
to look at …	гледати	gledati

to lose (umbrella, etc.)	изгубити	izgubiti
to love (sb)	волети	voleti
to make a mistake	грешити	grešiti
to meet (vi, vt)	сусрести се	susresti se
to miss (school, etc.)	пропустити	propustiti

30. Verbs. Part 3

to obey (vi, vt)	потчинити се	potčiniti se
to open (vt)	отворити	otvoriti
to participate (vi)	учествовати	učestvovati
to pay (vi, vt)	платити	platiti
to permit (vt)	дозволити	dozvoliti

to play (children)	играти се	igrati se
to pray (vi, vt)	молити се	moliti se
to promise (vt)	обећати	obećati
to propose (vt)	предлагати	predlagati
to prove (vt)	доказати	dokazati
to read (vi, vt)	читати	čitati

to receive (vt)	примити	primiti
to rent (sth from sb)	изнајмити	iznajmiti
to repeat (say again)	поновити	ponoviti
to reserve, to book	резервисати	rezervisati
to run (vi)	трчати	trčati

to save (rescue)	спасити	spasiti
to say (~ thank you)	рећи	reći
to see (vt)	видети	videti
to sell (vt)	продавати	prodavati
to send (vt)	послати	poslati
to shoot (vi)	пуцати	pucati

to shout (vi)	викати	vikati
to show (vt)	показати	pokazati
to sign (document)	потписати	potpisati
to sing (vi)	певати	pevati
to sit down (vi)	сести	sesti

to smile (vi)	осмехнути се	osmehnuti se
to speak (vi, vt)	говорити	govoriti
to steal (money, etc.)	красти	krasti
to stop	прекинути	prekinuti
(please ~ calling me)		

| to study (vt) | студирати | studirati |

to swim (vi)	пливати	plivati
to take (vt)	узети	uzeti
to talk to ...	говорити са ...	govoriti sa ...
to tell (story, joke)	рећи	reći
to thank (vt)	захвалити	zahvaliti
to think (vi, vt)	мислити	misliti

to translate (vt)	преводити	prevoditi
to trust (vt)	веровати	verovati
to try (attempt)	покушати	pokušati
to turn (e.g., ~ left)	скренути	skrenuti
to turn off	угасити, искључити	ugasiti, isključiti

to turn on	укључити	uključiti
to understand (vt)	разумети	razumeti
to wait (vt)	чекати	čekati
to want (wish, desire)	хтети	hteti
to work (vi)	радити	raditi
to write (vt)	писати	pisati

Printed in Great Britain
by Amazon